How The

Connect With Us... And

Vice Versa.

By

Leanne Halyburton

Also by **Leanne Halyburton**

Daniel Beyond Death

Our Life Beyond Death - An Incredible Journey

You Wear It Well

Available worldwide on Amazon

https://amazon.co.uk/B075Z46WCR

Contacting Leanne online

spiritoflife@hotmail.co.uk

www.leannehalyburton.com

https://www.facebook.com/StoriesByLeanne

Contents

Chapter 1

See, feel, hear.

Many years ago, when I used to travel out to conduct my work, there was an occasion on which the lady of the house led me up a steep set of stairs to a converted loft. There was a small table and chairs set up, and the idea was that her guests - my customers - would join me, one at a time, to receive their consultation.

Now, this particular group was in no hurry, and there was a long wait between one customer descending the stairs and the next ascending; I was becoming a tad impatient, thinking, "I am going to be here all night if this carries on!" Suddenly, I became aware of a tingling pressure on my top lip, and the face of a little girl very close to my own - she had

1

just kissed me! I clearly heard the words, "can she *see* me?" and the child, holding onto the hand of an adult who was out of my vision, was gently led backward; as she realised that yes, I *could* see her, she smiled delightedly and waved. She appeared to be around six years old with dark, wavy hair tumbling to her shoulders, and the sweetest smile. I gave a little wave in return, and she faded away. I never discovered the identity of my lovely little visitor, but what really struck me was her excitement and wonder when she realised that I could see her, as if that was an oddity, an unusual occurrence. As if I was the 'ghost' in *her* world.

Something else happened, too, whilst I was cooling my heels in that loft; a man and woman silently climbed the stairs and sat on chairs (that were not actually there) placed in front of the wall opposite to where I was sitting. They appeared, for all the world, to be waiting for an appointment; they didn't acknowledge me and not a word passed between them. Minutes ticked by with no sign of my next customer, and I watched as the couple stood up and headed back down the stairs. "That was bloody odd!" I mused. Anyway, the awaited lady finally arrived... and the silent visitors returned, settling themselves down. I described them to her, and she was immediately emotional: "That's my mother and father!" she whispered. For the life of me, I cannot remember what was communicated that day, but I am happy to report that they didn't remain silent and that their daughter was really happy to hear from them.

There are many ways in which *we* connect with non-physical dimensions, and they with us. I believe that some form of communication is always at play, whether or not we are aware. I myself have developed the ability to see (known as clairvoyance) and to feel (known as clairsentience). I don't 'see' beings with my eyes as such; it is more like seeing with my mind… and not in solid form, as if they are here, in the physical world; they appear more like holograms, which makes some sense to me. This snippet from Wikipedia explains it well:

"Typically, a **hologram** is a photographic recording of a light field, rather than an image formed by a device without a lens."

Deceased people and spiritual entities don't have a physical body in the way that we do, and so they are creating and presenting an *energetic* image of themselves, as a way of connecting with us and producing 'evidence'. We operate in a dimension in which we recognise and make sense of things through the conscious senses, and any being that wishes to communicate with us has to be able to do so in a language that we recognise and understand (and vice versa, of course). I have heard mediums say that they see those they are communicating with as if they are as solid as you and me, and that might well be true for them... it just isn't for me. Having said that, I do remember suddenly waking one night to see a man standing beside the bed, level with my head - and he *did* appear to be solid. Even though I was bleary-eyed, I could see that he sported a thick beard and scruffy, dark hair, was wearing a blue, round-neck tee shirt, and trousers that were baggy at the knees - and, even though I couldn't see them, I knew for sure that he was wearing tatty grey socks and no shoes. He was staring at *me*, too, and I swear that that is what woke me up! However, within seconds he disappeared and I still can't say for sure whether he was just a figment of my imagination or an actual non-physical entity. I had no idea who he was and still don't... but I picked up on a strong sense of irritability and grumpiness!

However, seeing is only one aspect of how it all works for me; *feeling* is the most important part of the process. And, when I say feeling, I don't just mean happy, sad, hot, cold etc.

I wish I could explain it more clearly (and I *have* tried to do so many times): there is a knowingness that comes through feeling, an instant understanding that emanates from within my mind. If I were to describe it in physical terms, I would say that it is kind of like a liquid that drips into the centre of my head and then spreads out. I find the feeling more informative and interesting than the seeing; the seeing without the feeling would be akin to gazing upon lifeless, cardboard cutouts, and I wouldn't enjoy that. I like to experience the essence of the communicator, to feel how they feel, and to understand who they were/are as a soul.

However, in the world of mediumship, the way in which I work isn't always what the customer is hoping for, and I have no problem being upfront about this. I do not consider myself to be the greatest medium on the planet, although I have had some satisfying results and a respectable number of happy customers. I am unable to say things like, "I have a connection with your Uncle Bob here; he was 63 years old when he passed, and he lived at number 23 Park Grove, and he loved Manchester United football team." I remember one Scottish medium claiming in the press that unless a reader can come up with names and other such specific details, then they aren't the real deal. Well, many would agree with him, but you can only be open to communication in the way that you are able to receive it... and, often, it is the seemingly most insignificant detail that can be the most meaningful to a grieving customer. I always gave the best I could, over a period of 25 years - and, I say *gave* because I no longer do much in the way of mediumship these days - but it never felt enough to me. I always wanted to be able to see, feel, and provide *more*!

What I *could* and did do with the skills I developed was to physically describe the soul with whom I was connecting, and express what I was feeling about them - their personality, their way of looking at life, and how they were, just prior to their passing. And, of course, I would explain all that was communicated to me in terms of 'messages'. I didn't tend to automatically know who they were, as in mother, father etc; I would simply pass on all of the information that I was able to receive and decipher, and the customer would usually have no difficulty in recognising the communicator. However, I came to the conclusion that it made more sense to be able to 'tune in' directly, and so I started to ask, "who is it, specifically, that are you hoping to make a connection with today?" This enabled me to make what I jokingly referred to as a 'cosmic phone call'... and it proved to be very effective! I would send out my thoughts to the requested loved one, and, more often than not, a connection was made… and usually *other* connections, too. Some people see this as 'cheating', believing that it is the medium's job to be able to know exactly who they wish to make a link with *and* provide the consultation; after 20 plus years, I had no interest in being 'tested' before I could get on with my work. I was always more invested in the results than in how many marks out of ten I might be awarded! I am aware that many mediums say that they have no control over who 'comes through', and that 'spirit' chooses. Again, for them, I am sure that that is true; it just isn't the way that I see it, or how I work. No-one is right, and no-one is wrong; it just comes down to personal style and preference. And, in case anyone wonders, I would only ask for the relationship of the deceased to the customer, *or* the first name and age at the time of passing. I didn't go looking things up, and even if I did try, it wouldn't have been effective because it wouldn't have provided me with the kind of information I was interested in.

So far, I have been talking about myself and how I learned to connect with non-physical souls. But, what about you? The wonderful thing about clairsentience is that we all possess the skill, whether or not we recognise it. We all feel our way through life; we all sense things; we all sometimes just *know* something without understanding *how* we know it. You might not be working as a professional medium, but that doesn't mean that you aren't clairsentient - you are! However, you may also find - with a little experimenting - that you are also clairvoyant and have a strong ability to 'see' with your mind, or you might discover that you are clairaudient, and able to 'hear'. The late, much-loved Doris Stokes delivered most of her work clairaudiently, which worked extremely well for her and those with whom she worked.

The chances are high that you will have strongly sensed the presence of someone who isn't physically there; you will have 'picked up' certain feelings from others around you, maybe without even realising; you will have found that a particular person suddenly entered your mind and stayed there, for no obvious reason; you will have been aware of the 'energetic sense' of an unfamiliar room or building you ventured into, in either a pleasant way or an uncomfortable way. This is *you* knowing stuff through feeling, and it is the same ability that is used by mediums. It isn't a gift that only a select few possess: it is something that *everyone* has been endowed with - a skill that can definitely be developed and strengthened.

Chapter 2

Weird... but completely true!

I was going to explain to you how I started to develop my ability to intuitively see and feel, thinking that it might be helpful to you... and then I remembered something that I haven't thought about for quite some time - something that is probably going to sound weird, not to mention entirely invented by a disturbed mind! However, I promise you that what I am going to tell you is absolutely true, *and* relevant to the title of this book.

I started to consciously work on energetic development around 1990, but toward the mid 90's I took it more seriously (eventually leading me to abandon my career in advertising sales to become a full-time intuitive consultant). In the meantime, I organised a little office in the corner of my bedroom, which became the setting for my strange story.

I had read a book about automatic writing and decided to give it a try. I would sit with an open notepad, pen poised as if to write… and wait. It didn't take very long for the pen to start writing, with me doing nothing more than holding it loosely, ballpoint resting lightly on the paper. At first, it was nothing more than scribble, but I persevered - and actual words and sentences started to appear. I came up with questions to ask, and answers that were not consciously known to me were supplied. At the time, I had developed an idea for a magazine for teens and was working on the editorial content, as well as drumming up advertising revenue. Through this, I came to know a young man and woman who were involved in youth work, and I would sometimes visit their office for a cup of tea and a catch-up. I told them all about my little hobby, and they were fascinated: "do it for us!" they begged… and so I did. I sat with my pad and pen and invited them to ask questions to which I couldn't possibly know the answer. I won't go into detail, but suffice to say my new friends were utterly blown away. In fact, they were shocked, and so was I. Where *was* this information coming from??

Increasingly, it felt to me that I was dealing with an actual communicator, and so I asked for their name - which was duly supplied via the automatic writing. I now have no memory of that name but *do* remember that it sounded 'foreign' to me, a name I was unfamiliar with. Even my friends started to talk about 'him' as if they knew him: "what does ***** have to say, today? Can I ask him a question?"

But then, there came about a new and strange development. I received a written message from someone who claimed to be called Connor Ross, a young man who had lived in East Kilbride, Scotland, and who had passed as a result of cancer. He told me that he wanted to get in touch with his widow, Louise, who was staying with his father... and he gave me the address. I rang directory enquiries, expecting them to say that they had nothing listed; instead, they informed me that the name of the person at that address was actually Rossi, not Ross - and that it was an ex-directory (unlisted) telephone number. They were not allowed to give it out.

I was gobsmacked. Okay, the name was slightly different... but the man actually existed... and the address

11

was correct! I returned to my pad and explained the situation - and was given the name and address of a neighbour to contact. Once again I called directory enquiries, and once again there was one slight inaccuracy: the lady in question *did* exist, but the number of her house was different. They gave me her phone number, and I called, explaining that I was trying to get in touch with Mr Rossi, and was hoping that she would be kind enough to take *my* number and pop it through his door. I can't remember how I explained having *her* details, but she was a lovely lady, and did as I asked.

When Mr Rossi called me, my face was as red as a stoplight, and my hands were shaking; he was going to think I was head-case... a stalker, even. Stammering and stuttering, I asked if he was the father of Connor, who had sadly passed from cancer and was the late husband of Louise. He immediately and emphatically said *no*... he did not have a deceased son and had never heard of Connor Rossi. Embarrassed and deflated, I quickly apologised, before ringing off. Luckily, he didn't ask me why I wanted to know this stuff, so I didn't have to explain that some invisible entity had sent me on a wild goose chase! But still, there was so much that was correct. I have never, ever been to East Kilbride, and had never heard the name Connor Rossi until that time. It was highly unnerving... and yet massively impressive, at the same time!

However, that wasn't quite the end of it all. I chewed it over and eventually went back to my pad in the early hours of the morning, writing about what had happened, and demanding an explanation. Once again my pen took on a life of its own, and a telephone number appeared on the page. Maybe this was where I was going to find the answer, but I certainly couldn't call *anyone* in the wee small hours. I went back to bed and tried to sleep; as soon as it was an acceptable time to make a phone call, I dialled that number - and *this* is what I heard:

"Hello, Scottish Widows Life Insurance And Pensions, can I help you?"

I slammed the phone down and knew for sure that I had been played like a fiddle! A Scottish guy looking for his widowed wife? The *Scottish Widows* Company? What a hilarious joke - I *don't* think! I realised that I had unwittingly become the plaything of... well, I don't know *what* it was. I was exhausted and vowed never again to communicate with my tormentor. It didn't give up easily, though. For days after, my hand would periodically buzz and vibrate, and I just knew that it was trying to get me to communicate again. However, I had finally had enough, and set out to learn how to use my intuitive ability in a safer, more sustainable way. Despite the craziness, I know that I will always retain a sense of eerie wonderment that such an experience was even possible! I can't say for sure whether it was a 'dark' entity trying to gain control of my mind, or just a very mischievous soul who was having a giggle at my naive expense. Either way, I wasn't willing to hang around to find out! You can see why this genuinely truthful story deserves to be included in a book about the ways in which we can connect with the 'dead' - and the ways in which *they* can connect with *us*!

Chapter 3

How I began to develop my intuitive skills – properly!

I would settle the children into bed at night, dim the light, and sit at a table with a lit candle in front of me. I would relax my mind and body, whilst gazing into the flame, blinking naturally, rather than staring.

When I felt ready, I would close my eyes and attempt to picture the flame in my mind; with a little practice it became easier to do. What I was actually doing was training myself to project an image upon the screen of my mind - something that would prove to be very useful to me, further down the line. I progressed to picturing myself sitting at a small table, with a lit candle in front of me, and an empty chair opposite… and I waited, wondering if anyone would show up and join me!

My first visitor was a little boy who had very much been on my mind. He had been the victim of murder, in a case that was utterly devastating and heartbreaking, and the newspapers had recently been awash with reports about the inquest. I, like many others, was grieving the loss of a child and the shocking nature of the crime… but I genuinely wasn't expecting to *see* him. However, whilst sitting at the little table in my mind, I was surprised to see a small boy plonk himself down in the empty chair - and immediately attempt to blow out my candle! "Don't do that," I laughingly chided, when suddenly the scene changed, and the boy was standing with his back to me, a football tucked under one arm… and then he turned, smiling, gave a little wave, and was gone. I was blown away, mostly because I recognised him: he was the child so savagely taken from this world… and he was letting me know that he was safe and happy! I felt so much better after that experience, as if a weight had been lifted from my shoulders. Some will say that it was just the workings of my own mind, something I unconsciously created in order to find peace… and they may possibly be right. All I can say is that it felt genuinely real to me, and that it was the beginning of something that was to play a massive role in my life. There were other visitors after that, and, eventually, I no longer needed the imaginary little room *or* the candle. I was able to simply close my eyes, clear my mind, and wait for images to take shape and form on the screen of my mind - always accompanied by a sense, and a collection of feelings. Of course, I have made it sound effortless and easy here, but obviously that is not true; I have worked hard throughout the years in a hands-on way, whilst continuing to develop and refine my skills… and I still see myself as a work in progress! However - it all *began* with a tealight candle and a beautiful little boy! And, for those who haven't read my book, Our Life Beyond Death - An Incredible Journey, I will explain a little about my personal beliefs about the connection between physical life and death, and the ways in which we continue to communicate.

I believe that each of us is a soul; a unique, individual shard of the great, creative source of life (call it God, the Universe, the Mothership… whatever works for you). I believe that the only thing we take with us when we leave this physical experience is our spirit. And, that our spirit is the sum total of everything we have become as a result of this incarnation; it is a reflection of our overall relationship with life - a record of the perceptions, beliefs, and general attitude that we hold at the time of our passing. We, the soul, absorb the contents of our spirit, as does the 'collective' soul; nothing is ever lost or meaningless - it *all* counts. Of course, these are *my* beliefs, and I am not suggesting that you should see things in exactly the same way. I have no interest in persuading or converting anyone. I am only sharing some of what I have experienced, and explaining my personal conclusions; hopefully, the reader will find something of interest within these pages... or, at the very least, feel that they have been mildly entertained!

I also believe that our connection with non-physical souls is *energetic*; the link is always mind to mind. Some of the communication has to be processed through the conscious senses, such as sight and hearing, which makes communication a little easier for us. However, much more can be given and received through emotional/intuitive sense and feeling. As previously mentioned, I am not just referring to sensation such as hot or cold, or emotions like happy or sad; there is a knowingness that can be silently passed from one mind to another, without the need for words or explanation. Sounds tricky, doesn't it, as if it must be incredibly hard to master? Well, here's the good news: we are all *already* doing this, in everyday life!

There isn't one way of communicating with human beings, and another way of communicating with the 'deceased'... it is basically the same principle, but with a bit of adaptation and a few obvious limitations. We *feel* our way through life, often without even realising that we are doing so. We can suddenly experience a strong sense of something about a loved one who lives on the other side of the planet, or, find ourselves thinking about someone we haven't seen for years - only to bump into them on the street or receive an unexpected phone call. We can sometimes see *through* what another person is determinedly presenting to the outer world, and gain a glimpse of their inner world (or engine room, as I call it), even when others appear to be oblivious. We are accustomed to using our ears and our eyes, which often leads us to operate on busy autopilot - reacting to life, rather than responding to it - consciously unaware of all that our *unconscious mind* is studiously observing and recording. We know so much more than we know that we know... if you see what I mean! Learning to communicate with life - and death - through feeling, is one of the most interesting and important skills that a human soul can invest time and energy in. It allows us to read our fellow human beings more effectively, *and* to communicate with non-physical souls, albeit in a lesser, more limited way. As with all skills in life, some are more naturally aligned than others; but, also as with all skills in life, the willingness to learn, combined with consistent practice, can only ever lead to improvement.

Sadly, unnecessary fluff and drama are often attached to the world of mediumship, which has led it to be misunderstood and disrespected... and therefore *not* explored in a fair and objective way. Some people claim that intuitives, psychics, and mediums, are 'gifted' with a sixth sense, but I don't agree. That would imply that only a select few possess intuitive capacity... and that everyone else *doesn't*. This belief is enough to discourage those who would love to test and develop their own skills, but who fear that they aren't good enough - that they aren't 'gifted' enough. Once again, I hasten to add that this is only the way in which I myself view the subject, and I am sure that many folk will disagree with me... and here is a little story about someone who *did*!

A number of years ago, I wrote an article about my work for a local newspaper, which included my opinion about people (not) being 'gifted' with a sixth sense. Shortly after it was published, a fortune teller I vaguely knew suddenly began to blank me, making it clear that she was deliberately ignoring me - and I had absolutely no idea why, until a friend commented: "Oh, you've really upset L***!" I said, "*have* I? Why, what have I done?"

Apparently, she'd read the article and was highly offended by my assertion that intuitive ability is something that is natural to everyone, rather than being bestowed upon a select few. It still didn't make sense to me, though. "Why would *that* upset her so much?" I queried, and my friend explained: "because she absolutely prides herself on what she considers to be her gift. She took it very personally indeed!" Oh dear. I don't think she ever did speak to me again, and I didn't apologise; I was sorry that she was upset, of course, and I made a mental note to be more mindful of how I expressed things in the future... but also, to make it clear that my beliefs are just *that*: mine. Maybe I did that in the article, anyway - I can't remember now. But, isn't it fascinating, how different we human souls are, and how diverse our beliefs? It is what makes life so challenging... and yet so incredibly interesting, too!

Chapter 4

Don't Fear The Feeling...

My niece died when she was 13, having battled a long-term health problem that caused her to undergo many medical procedures. In the end, she simply slipped away from this world, and those who loved her were left to grieve an immeasurable loss. I remember thinking, "I never want to feel this kind of pain again as long as I live."

However, she wasn't about to just skip off and leave us to our own devices - she wanted to let us know that she was finally free of the almost life-long pain and restriction, for *good*... but also, that she was still very much within reach. One night, only days after she had passed, I was lying in bed, eyes closed, silent tears pouring down my cheeks... and I felt her kiss me. I knew for sure that it was her because the kiss was accompanied by an incredibly strong (albeit fleeting) sense of *her*. There was no mistaking it. And, of course, her loving gesture really soothed and comforted me, if only for that night.

I did see her several times, though always briefly, within the months following her departure from this physical dimension; she usually appeared as she was when around the age of four or five... and always wearing her old, beloved dressing gown! However, as wonderful as that was, *feeling* her presence - the unique essence of *her* - was even more powerful and reassuring than *seeing* her. A sighting can come and go in the blink of an eye - but a sense lingers, leaving something of itself behind... an emotional connection for us to savour and treasure.

The problem is, though, that many of us struggle to trust that what we are feeling is actually 'real'; we fear that it is nothing more than our imagination, fuelled by sadness and yearning, or by wishful thinking. All I can say is that if it feels real to you, in a loving way, then it *is* real. No, it cannot be proved to be real in the way in which serious sceptics claim that it *should* be - but neither can it be *disproved*, in an absolute, concrete, beyond-question kind of way! There are those who claim that it can be - and, in fact, *has* been - and that science holds all of the answers to everything. As far as I can see, it doesn't, and I feel that they are missing something.

We human souls are navigating our way through a dimension in which everything has an opposite (with some degree of blurring): night and day, hot and cold, young and old, happy and sad... birth and death, physics and metaphysics, matter and antimatter. I am not a scientist (obviously), though I am absolutely in awe of scientific minds, wishing that I could even begin to know and understand a tiny portion of what they do - but without sacrificing my relationship with the metaphysical world. It makes no sense to me that it has to be one or the other... we need both, surely, in order to be able to further develop our understanding of our universe, our dimension - our very lives, in fact? The fact is, if *we* can't feel something that someone else *can*, it doesn't automatically make them delusional or crazy. I am aware that there are poor souls who have officially been diagnosed with the kind of mental health problem that leads to them to see and hear things that probably aren't there, but right now I am talking about those of us who are deemed to be largely of sound and healthy mind.

So, there is a good chance that you will be persuaded by others that you are only imagining a sensory connection with a deceased loved one, and you are likely to tell yourself that it *is* only your own desperate imagination at play. You might even feel afraid that a loved one will show themselves to you and that it will be a frightening experience (believe me, your loved ones would never, ever want to scare you). Or, you might just be afraid to open yourself to 'spirit', in case you attract a dark energy! Believe it or not, this is actually a pretty common fear… and it isn't a completely unreasonable one, either! And, in line with that thought, here comes another little story, one that illustrates the kind of fear human souls experience when it comes to talking with the 'dead'…

Several years ago, when I used to travel out to work with groups of customers, I was booked by a young woman who lived in a small apartment with her little boy. As I walked through the door, she nervously blurted out, "my friend says that I shouldn't have someone like you in my home!" "Really," I asked. "And why is that?" "Because I have a child," she replied. I was a bit confused by the conversation, to say the least (after all, it was *she* who had asked me to attend - I wasn't exactly forcing my way in!), so I could only respond with, "and… ?", even though I should have known what was coming. "Well," she muttered, "you might leave something behind!" By 'something' I assumed that she meant a dark entity… a lost and angry ghost! ! "Ah, I see," I calmly replied. "Well, let me ask you something. Do you honestly believe that any of your deceased friends or relatives *really* wish to spend eternity in a flat in North Wales? And also, if I *am* going to leave something behind, then I am afraid that I am going to have to charge you double!" She saw the funny side, laughed, and we got on with things - and, as far as I know, when I left I took all of my demons with me!

However, I could kind of understand her concerns; the unknown is often a terrifying concept. We have a yearning to know more, to connect with non-physical souls, whilst at the same time being afraid of what that might lead to or open up. It's a tough one, for sure. However, it depends upon how we approach the situation, and what we involve ourselves with. As long as we are grounded, and operating from a balanced mindset, there is nothing of a metaphysical nature that can hurt us. We always have the power to switch off, to step back, if we feel that we are getting into something that is causing us to feel uncomfortable or negatively interfering with our life. You can see from chapter 2 that I was able to break a connection that was clearly playing games with me… that whatever or whoever was behind it could only continue if I *allowed* it to. I still can't decide whether it was a negatively intentioned entity, a merely playful, mischievous one… *or*, one whose intention was to teach me something very important. In hindsight, I think it was probably the third option. I was blown away by the whole experience, by what was actually possible… but I had to ultimately reach the stage at which I was standing on my own two feet, metaphorically speaking. I have no regrets; it was a fascinating though unsettling - and sometimes embarrassing! - experience, that taught me a huge amount, including the fact that I always have the power of control over my own mind. I have a healthy respect for the 'dark side' (there is no point in pretending that it doesn't exist; there can be no light without dark, and vice versa) - but I *choose* not to involve myself with it, unless absolutely necessary!

If you are in the process of developing your own intuitive capacity, or would very much like to, then you have to become increasingly open to 'feeling', because that is the language of the soul. Seeing and hearing are important tools, but, on their own, they are not enough. The good news is, the more we practice, the more adept we become… we learn how to trust our own interpretation of what it is that we are feeling, seeing, and hearing. I used to believe that there was a difference in the ways in which mediums and psychics operate, that somehow they employed different methods of working. However, experience taught me that it all comes down to being able to 'read' through feeling, whether our focus is the living or the deceased. If I explain how I myself work, it might make things clearer.

When I am 'tuning in' to a living, breathing soul, where a general consultation is concerned, I usually only have their first name and age, provided by email (I no longer work with people on a face to face basis). I sit, eyes closed, and clear my mind before focusing on the person in question… and then I wait. First, a sense of that person begins to develop, and I sit with it for as long as it takes; I might feel that they are currently angry, sad, doubtful, fearful, lonely, frustrated, or just plain stuck. I relax with whatever I am feeling, and wait to see if it develops any further, or changes in a notable way. This lets me know whether the customer is only feeling this way right now, at this moment in time, *or*, whether it has become an habitual state of mind. Next, a series of little images flash across the screen of my mind, be they still-frames or moving clips... only ever snippets, never a full movie! I now have a sense of the person I am 'reading', plus a collection of images, and this is my starting point for the consultation. The images alone are not enough to allow me to really connect with the customer, and here is a simple example that will explain what I mean: say I 'see' an image of a man holding an axe, but without any accompanying feeling; it could be that he is about to commit a murder, or it could be that he is about to chop wood so that he can make a nice, cozy fire! However, if I *also* experience a sense of dread and fear, I know that this man's intentions are not good, and I can then actively attempt to follow it along and see where it leads me.

Now, say I am attempting to make a deliberate connection with a non-physical soul (as opposed to the random, unexpected visits that sometimes occur!), the process is exactly the same. I generally ask for the first name of the deceased, and/or their relationship to the customer, and that is what I bring to mind, asking to make a link (or, as previously mentioned, a 'cosmic phone call'!). Generally, I will see the person first, followed by the sense of them... and we move forward from that point, communicating through a combination of feelings and images. I am not saying that this is exactly how *every* medium works, but I still firmly believe that it is impossible for anyone to make a productive connection *without* clairsentience. And, the good thing is, we are all naturally clairsentient beings... we just often allow fear and doubt to get in the way, clouding our vision and our openness! We have to be patient, and we have to persist... and, if we are serious about all of this stuff, we need to be willing to practice!

So, you can see that there really isn't too much to be afraid of, where energetic communication is concerned! This is my rule of thumb: if we are operating from a reasonably healthy mindset, and our intention is genuinely positive, it is highly unlikely that we will become 'possessed' by some errant, dark soul! And, I have to tell you, the living are way more likely to drain you, mentally and emotionally, *and* even leave some of their unhappy energy behind! In the days when I worked with people on a face to face basis, there were times when I actually became ill as a result of dealing with a (thankfully) small number of customers. I remember leaving one particular house feeling absolutely wretched, as if my inner world had been dragged out, trampled on, and trashed (and no, bubbles of light are *not* enough to provide protection from the kind of energy that can do that to you!). Science tells us that when two particles come together and then pull apart, they each leave something behind and they each take something away. Some people's inner world is so intense and messed-up, at the time that you are connecting with them, that they take a big chunk of your good stuff in return for a dollop of their sludge, misery, or rage. It is just the way it is, with life on planet Earth; sometimes we are the givers, and sometimes we are the takers. And, some souls are mostly always the givers, and some are mostly always the takers. We just have to figure it out as we are going along, and look after ourselves.

Going back to fearing the 'feeling', I haven't decided whether it is scarier for the rookie communicator to suddenly *see* something, or to become aware of a particular feeling that makes no immediate sense! We all know what it is like to be quietly getting on with things, all on our own… only to develop a strong suspicion that someone is watching us! The good thing about being able to sense a change in the energy around us is that it is usually easy to figure out whether we feel okay with it, or whether we are unsettled… scared, even. Trust me, there is *always* something going on around us that we are mostly oblivious to… but, sometimes, and for certain reasons, we become *aware* - and once we become aware, we tend to feel, or see, or hear, things that we previously couldn't. It seems that people often believe that there are only two places where souls can exist: either here, on planet Earth, or, on the 'other side'. I think that that is probably a little simplistic; it makes more sense to me that there are actually many dimensions of existence, all occupying the same space at the same time - and at different levels of awareness! Also, it seems reasonable to conclude that the dimensions sometimes overlap, which would explain sudden paranormal activity and hauntings. I suppose then, from that point of view, the 'other side' is just a collective term for every other dimension of existence, apart from life on Earth. Mind-boggling, isn't it... especially if it's anywhere near true?

Chapter 5

So many ways to stay in touch…

Where white feathers are concerned, I used to be pretty sceptical… and unfairly so. Just because the idea of them being messages from 'spirit' didn't resonate with *me*, it didn't mean that I was right and that everyone else was wrong. I remember becoming frustrated with a good friend who was forever seeing white feathers and pointing them out as 'signs'. "Oh, for goodness sake," I told her, "we live on an island, surrounded by seawater, with a zillion seagulls flying overhead at any given moment in time. I don't think it's a mystery where the feathers are coming from!" Ouch, how brutal was that? I suppose I was so keen not to buy into spiritual fluff that I went a bit too far the other way. And then, one day, whilst

33

walking through the woods with our beloved old dog (who is now, very sadly for us, deceased), something suddenly fluttered down and swept past my shoulder. I quickly turned to investigate... only to see a soft, pale grey feather lying on the pathway behind me. I had been walking beneath a clump of trees, shaded by their branches - which I studiously examined for evidence of a shedding bird...but, there was none. Of course, the feather could have been caught up in the leaves and dislodged by a gentle breeze, but it was the *way* that it fell, almost brushing the side of my face before dancing past my shoulder, that really made me stop and think. Okay, it was grey and not white (that's typical of me, isn't it? Always got to be different), but it genuinely felt 'special' to me, somehow. I had a habit of conversing with the great force of life on those walks, of chewing things over and asking questions in my mind, and I think that that just might have been an affectionate, teasing gesture (writing this reminded me to check the tray upon which I laid out all of the heart-shaped stones I collected on our walks along the beach next to the woods, and there it *is* - I actually kept it!).

Another good friend believes that a robin in her garden is a little message from her father... a meaningful way of saying hello. Of course, there are reasons behind her belief, she didn't simply decide one day that her deceased dad had taken up residence in a little red-breasted bird! If something touches us deeply, if somehow it feels real to us and just seems to make sense... then it *is* real. We receive communication in the way in which *we* are able to, in a way that reaches *us*. It isn't the same for everyone, it isn't a one-size-fits-all kind of thing. I tend to receive snippets through the words of songs and books, because they are meaningful to me and I pay attention to them. It might not always be some great message from a deceased loved one - it might just be a bit of encouragement, or a helping hand... for which I am always grateful! For example, just today, my partner and I were struggling with technology, trying to sort something out, and we needed a particular password. Now, I remembered that my son had sent this pass-word to me, months ago, but held out no hope of finding it as we have texted many, many times since. I said, "well, I will just have to call him later, when he has finished work", as I did one quick, cursory scroll with my thumb... and right there, in the centre of the screen, appeared the password! There was another occasion on which I was really keen to find the phone number of a woman I knew I had visited in a professional capacity, maybe a year or two earlier. I suspected that she was behind something dubious and I needed to check the number against one that had been used to call me. I had no recollection of dates and so believed that I would have to go through my old diary, page by page. But then, one night, whilst lying in bed and ruminating over the situation, a voice in my mind said, "go and look at your diary!" Although it was late, I thought, "okay, but this had better not be a waste of time", and I crept downstairs, picked up my diary from the telephone table, opening it randomly... at the very page upon which I had written the said woman's number! As it happens, I was right... she *was* responsible for the dodgy dealings! So, if I see these kinds of occurrences as forms of communication from non-physical sources, then who am I to decide that white feathers *aren't?* No-one, that's who!

Anyway, what are some of the *other* ways in which the 'dead' connect with us? Well, through the services of a medium, through dreams, through meaningful, familiar songs and words, through our own senses (conscious and intuitive), and even through sudden sightings of a stranger who strongly reminds us of our lost loved one. Yes, I know that some will say, "oh, anyone can make *anything* fit if they really want to", and I couldn't argue with that; however, as I said earlier, if a connection honestly feels real to us then it *is* real. There is no need to convince or persuade anyone else to see it our way. There are those who advise the grieving to move on, to get back to 'normal' as quickly as possible, and who believe that they shouldn't be encouraged to hold on to the past; however, no-one ever gets over the loss of a loved one… they just learn to live with it, in their own way and in their own time. Everything is different when someone we love dies. Nothing is ever the same again. And yes, with the slow passing of time, the pain dulls a little and we do smile again, do enjoy life again… but there is always an empty space within us that can never be filled - and it is all of *this* that becomes our new normal. To be left completely adrift would be soul-destroying; to believe that that is it - that there is nothing but oblivion for our loved ones and ultimately for ourselves, would be too much to bear, for most human beings at least. There are those who are highly vocal in their attempt to convert others into accepting that consciousness and awareness do not survive physical death, and that our deceased loved ones simply cease to exist in any way, shape, or form. They believe that anyone who doesn't see things in the same way that they do is naive, stupid, delusional, and, even worse, hanging onto a fantasy that is being fed by unscrupulous con-artists just looking to make a fast buck. And yes, those quick-talking, attention-seeking con-artists *do* exist, for sure; not everyone who works within the spiritual arena is genuine and above board. We all know that, and anyone who has read my book, Our Life

Beyond Death - An Incredible Journey, is already aware of my views about the super-cynics *and* the spiritual bottom-dwellers! However, doesn't every industry have its heroes and its villains? For example, I personally haven't had one single positive experience with a solicitor, ever; there has always been hassle and poor communication; they don't get back to you when they say they will; they give big attitude when questioned; they take no responsibility for what turns out to be poor guidance and advice... and yet they still expect to be paid! However, that doesn't mean that every solicitor on the planet should automatically be tarred with the same brush. There will be excellent, hard-working, committed ones amongst them (I still believe... I *have* to believe!). I know that you can't compare a solicitor with someone who 'talks to the dead' (although the cynics would probably argue that you *can*, because, in their opinion, both are equally dodgy!). The point is, there are great doctors, and lousy doctors; there are warm, dedicated nurses, and bad-attitude nurses; there are friendly, chatty bus drivers, and miserable-as-sin bus drivers; as I said, every industry has its heroes and its villains. Anyway, back to some of the ways in which non-physical souls communicate with us... *and* why it isn't always easy to understand or accept what they are expressing!

I had a not-so settled childhood, and there was a period of many years in which I didn't see my mother or even know of her whereabouts - and I am explaining this purely because of the following story.

Some years after my mother passed, my own family were facing a very difficult situation, and I knew that the next day could potentially bring really bad news. I stepped outside into the darkness of the night, brooding and worrying, and called out loud, "Mum, what's going to happen tomorrow?" I had never tried to make any kind of connection with her before, so you can see how desperate I was feeling. I saw her, briefly (or at least a hazy image of her), standing several feet away, and in her outstretched hands was a bunch of daisies - all with brown, wilted petals. Gee, thanks, a bunch of dead flowers! I had no idea what it meant, not even sure whether or not I had dreamed it up, and so I slunk back into the house, dreading the following day.

As it happened, the worst that *could* have occurred didn't, and we were so relieved that we went to a nice little hotel for a celebratory lunch. Whilst the others were finishing their drinks, I stood at the front entrance, breathing in the air, and gazing out across the sea... and it suddenly hit me: the hotel garden was filled with Michaelmas daisies - all of which were dying, brown, and wilted. I was genuinely shocked, because I suddenly recognised what she'd been trying to convey: that when I saw the dying daisies, everything would be okay! I thanked her, of course, but was once again reminded of how easy it is to dismiss and forget about something that makes no immediate sense to us. I have seen customers do this time and time again; it is, unfortunately, just the way we human souls tend to operate. If I hadn't actually *noticed* those withered flowers, I wouldn't have ever understood her message. How many other insightful little nuggets have I missed, throughout the years? Hundreds, I imagine... possibly even thousands. Many of us end up functioning on autopilot, oblivious to anything but the absolute obvious. We are all guilty of it, to one degree or another, but we *can* become habitually more aware, with conscious effort.

And it isn't just about not recognising or acknowledging the manifestation of a message or prediction... it is also about the stuff that we *forget!* Following the death of my niece, I visited a medium I had never seen before (or since), and she explained that she was aware of a little girl who used to love dancing - and I shook my head, genuinely baffled. All I could

think of at that moment in time was how ill she had been...
what the hell did dancing have to do with it? Afterwards, I felt
like shaking myself until my teeth rattled! How could I have
forgotten? In between the bad bouts she *did* get on with life...
and she had been a keen Morris dancer! I had become so
caught up in the emotion that I had re-written history! The
medium also said other things that made no immediate sense
to me, such as the fact that she could see my niece linking my
arm and holding onto my wrist, something I had never
experienced with her. However, one of my sisters later told
me that she had done it with her, many times. Maybe she *did*
do it with me, too... I just couldn't bring it to mind. I swear,
we must drive the 'dead' mad with our poor memories and
our eagerness to deny anything that requires a little bit of time
and consideration! I have worked with some individuals who
have, in my opinion, been so rude to the communicator that
I have apologised on their behalf, silently advising the visitor
not to bother next time! One of the most common examples
would be when a customer would respond to a link with
something like, "well, that sounds just like my Uncle Fred.
Why would HE bother showing up, I didn't see him that
often!" In return, I would ask them, "so, if this gentleman was
still here, in the physical sense, and he walked through that
door right now, saying hello and giving you a little message,

would you treat him with the same disrespect?" Of course, that rarely went down well and was usually met with a glare and a shrug. I can genuinely understand and accept forgetfulness, especially when emotions are high... but there is no need for rudeness!

I remember another occasion on which I was giving a public demonstration to an audience seated cabaret-style around small tables. There was a rather well-built man sitting alone, fairly close to the stage, arms folded firmly across his chest. I spoke directly to him, describing an elderly lady I could see standing to his left, and explained how she had been, just prior to her passing, and also how she was when fit and well... giving out snippets of information as I interpreted them. He dismissed *everything* I said, without hesitation. Now, this is not a comfortable position for a medium to be in, onstage, and under the scrutiny of a roomful of silent strangers... but all was not lost. A woman, seated at another table, piped up with, "that's our grandma!" and I was confused, thinking that maybe I had muddled up the connection. However, it became apparent that she was the unresponsive man's sister, and I asked how it was that she, and her sister who was also present, recognised the lady when their brother couldn't. "Because he left home when he was quite young," she explained, "and he saw very little of her after that!" Phew, mystery solved (I could have kissed her!). I don't know why she showed herself alongside *him*, rather than the granddaughters who had remained in contact with her… but he did make himself look a bit awkward and silly, so maybe that was her way of teaching him a lesson!

Having said that, it isn't easy to trust that what we are seeing, feeling, or hearing, is real and authentic, and it isn't easy to trust a person just because they claim to be able to communicate with the deceased. A certain degree of scepticism is healthy, and it isn't wrong to reserve judgement until we have carefully considered the 'evidence'. And, ironically, it is sometimes an individual's desperate hope and need to receive something that they *can* believe that leads them to be so strongly resistant: the idea of being fooled or conned is too awful to contemplate. Once such lady left me feeling deflated, inadequate and - quite frankly - pretty angry, many years ago (though nowadays I am able to view it more kindly).

I had worked my way through her consultation, believing that I had done fairly well, having made links with her sister, a niece, and her grandfather. My ego fully expected her to thank me for having done such a good job… but oh, how wrong it was! She gathered her things together and sighed deeply, bitterly announcing, "well, I had high hopes, but just like all of the others you haven't helped me at all. And now I am going to have to face yet *another* sleepless night… the same as *always*." I was shocked, and felt myself crumbling inside. "I don't understand," I stammered. "What has caused you to feel this way?" She glared at me. "If you had been able to give me the nickname that my sister used to call me by, I would have been able to believe. But you didn't, and all that has happened is that I have just wasted more time and money." And with that, she left. I took it personally because I was struggling with huge self-doubt, and the toll taken by consistent exposure to sad, grieving, and sometimes difficult customers… as *well* as dealing with some pretty big problems in my own life, too. Gradually, I came to understand that some people really need the services of a bereavement counsellor, rather than a medium, and that even if it *feels* personal, it usually isn't. It was all part of my apprenticeship, a steep learning curve that eventually helped me to develop a thicker skin - thank goodness!

Chapter 6

A bit of woo-woo for you...

I have been talking about how important *feeling* is, where spiritual communication (incoming and outgoing) is concerned. And there is something you can do that really does help to move your development along: tree hugging! Yes, I *have* hugged trees... and thoroughly enjoyed it (not when anyone else is around, of course; even I'm not that unselfconscious!). Trees definitely have their own unique energy field, as does everything else that exists in this world. I have hugged trees that have felt friendly and strong; I have hugged trees that have seemed more quiet and watchful. I have also picked up pebbles and shells, opening my mind to their history by holding them in my hand, closing my eyes, and clearing my mind... opening up the visual and sensory communication channels. Sometimes there has been very little; other times a scene has unfolded upon the screen of my mind, revealing snippets of the item's origins or past. Obviously, I don't have any way of knowing for sure whether what I am seeing and feeling is merely the workings of my own imagination, but it doesn't matter to me. I find it interesting, and it has definitely helped me to develop the senses that allow me to communicate with non-physical beings. And, the good thing is, it is something that anyone can do, anywhere. So, start hugging, and tuning into all of those interesting little things you find lying around in nature! The more we train ourselves to *feel* information, rather than relying purely upon what our conscious senses are presenting to us, the more intuitively adept we become.

We can also strengthen our ability to know through feeling by 'reading' objects such as rings, keys, watches… anything, in fact, that contains an imprint of the person who owns/owned it. This is known as psychometry (a belief that an object has an energy field from which it transfers information connected to its history; however, there is no *scientific* evidence to support its existence). Obviously, we are not communicating with the dead when we do this (although we can still pick up on the essence of someone who owned and used the object, but who has since passed). I have had some very impressive results with psychometry, and it can be highly entertaining for both observers *and* participants. In the days when I performed public demonstrations and stage shows, I would often explain to the audience that I was going to leave the room whilst whoever was assisting me collected a *specified* number of items (usually 6) on a tray; upon my return, I would 'tune into' and read them. Every single time, without fail, the collector would, in my absence, be mobbed - and I would return to find a tray piled high with rings, earrings, car and house keys, hair clips, combs, badges... you name it, it'd be on there! "Can nobody around here *count*?" I would quip, in mock annoyance... and the response would always be guilty laughter! Anyway, the point is, it is an excellent exercise for developing those intuitive 'muscles' that prove to be so helpful when attempting to connect with the 'dead'!

Chapter 7

Unbidden visitors...

Recently, we were driving past a horse riding establishment that I used to visit with my younger daughter - and I suddenly remembered the freckle-faced man whose presence was revealed by a Jack Russell terrier!

I was alone, heading across the car park toward the stables, when I became aware that the owner's little dog was leaping up and down, wagging its tail, and barking excitedly - at an empty vehicle. I stood and watched for a while, curious as to why the animal was behaving in such a weird way... and then I saw him. He was leaning against the side of the car, arms folded across his chest - and he was looking straight at me. Tall, fairly good build, thick auburn hair, and a healthy-looking freckled face! He appeared completely relaxed and at home, in his corduroy trousers, chunky sweater, and well-worn cap. In fact, if I remember rightly, he gave me a thumbs-up, as a cheeky gesture of acknowledgement. There was something mischievous about him, as if he found the whole situation amusing... and he seemed pleased that I could see him, as if he'd intended that all along. To be honest, if it hadn't been for that little dog, I *wouldn't* have seen him (animals are amazingly intuitive). Nothing more happened. I could hardly stand there staring at what was, to all intents and purposes, just a parked and empty car. I nodded to him, and then went about my business. I don't remember approaching the owner of the stables to tell her about the experience; I probably reckoned that it was better to keep it to myself, and avoid the risk of potential embarrassment to my daughter!

The question is, what did that non-physical, energetic being *want*? Was there a burning message that he was desperate to share with me? Did he require some kind of help from me? No, on both counts - or, at least, not that I am aware of. Sometimes, it seems, they just want to be seen...

The above story reminded me of another occasion when a 'visitor' deliberately made its presence known to me - and this one was a bit scary! I was in a pub with my now ex husband and our children, and we had just ordered a meal. They were larking around, playing a silly game, and for some reason I decided to secretly 'look' around the room to see if I could spot any non-physical energies - *and* I did (be careful what you wish for). The bar/restaurant had a number of floor to ceiling columns, with shelves halfway down upon which customers could place their glasses or cups. As my eyes scanned the room, I suddenly realised that there was a tall, dark-skinned man 'standing' at the column nearest to our table... and he raised a glass to me, grinning wickedly. Although handsome, there was something very unsettling about him, and a chill ran through me (not least because I had seen him before... but more of that later!) I immediately disconnected, and reminded myself to mind my own business in future! Again, there was no message, and no need for communication. Nevertheless, giving me that jolt clearly entertained him, in the way that jumping out at someone from behind a door and shouting "BOO" does!

Not *all* unbidden visitors are cheeky or unnerving, though. I was once walking through the wood with our beloved Tink (we have just had the first anniversary of her passing, a date I was dreading; however, I decided to celebrate her life, and the fact that we were lucky enough to have had her company for 15 years, rather than grieve her loss), and had reached my favourite part, a place where the river curved widely. I always took time there to enjoy the sight of bubbling water dancing around fallen logs and low, outstretched branches (once, two rooks were fighting in one of the overhanging trees, and tumbled into the water in front of me. They were almost carried away, panicking and flapping; I was just about to jump in when they managed to scrabble onto the bank, indignantly shaking out their soggy feathers!). As I turned back to the path, I became aware that an elderly lady was sitting on the painted wooden bench that faced the bend in the river. She smiled at me and patted the space next to her, inviting me to sit down. I hesitated for a moment, and went to walk on… but changed my mind. She was petite, very smartly dressed (all in black, but in a stylish rather than mournful way), and exuded an air of dignified calm. I cannot remember all that we talked about, as so often happens… the conversation tends to drift away, in the same way that dreams do, as we wake up. *Except* that she was Welsh, had always been a bit ahead of her time, loved music and dancing, and had enjoyed a great faith in God. I am sure that her name began with the letter A, but there was so much that simply faded from my consciousness as I said goodbye and continued my walk (with a grateful Tink, who had patiently been passing the time by sniffing amongst the grass and trees!). It was a pleasant and interesting interlude, and it got me thinking; maybe the 'deceased' sometimes simply enjoy a chat with the 'living'; or maybe they get a buzz out of the fact that they can be seen. I would imagine that these are pretty evolved or powerful entities, but I can't say for sure. And, here's another thought: what if it is *us* that are the unbidden visitors in *their* world(s)? What if it is us who are suddenly appearing in front of them, and not the other way round? It isn't beyond the realm of possibility, I imagine.

I have, throughout the years, experienced many brief glimpses of non-physical souls, but the sightings don't automatically lead to interaction. Sometimes a nod of greeting, or the polite lifting of a cap or hat… but, often, there is no acknowledgement at all, as if they either can't see me or have no interest in me. I don't tend to deliberately go looking nowadays, and anyway, it has all just become pretty 'normal'… a part of everyday life. Let's face it, I am certainly not the only human being who sees, hears, or feels the presence of 'dead people' - and just because some of us either *currently* can't, or are resistant to the idea, it doesn't mean that they aren't around us, sharing the same space, albeit experiencing a different level of awareness.

Every now and then, when I am in bed at night and on the verge of sleep, I will become aware that someone is trying to get my attention. This happened very recently, when I noticed the shadowy outline of a woman at the end of the bed. The name, 'Frances Whaley' flitted across the screen of my mind (which isn't a common occurrence - I tend to see and feel, more than hear). However, as there was no sense of urgency or need, and no obvious 'message', I drifted off to sleep. The following morning, I Googled the name, and a whole list of deceased Frances Whaley's came up, most of them in America. I had a vague memory of also hearing the name of a location, but I couldn't bring it to mind… I thought that it was somewhere in the UK. Anyway, that was about as far as I got, and I haven't seen or heard anything more from her. Maybe she was window shopping for a medium she felt comfortable with, or could get through to… and who wouldn't doze off! As I said, there was absolutely no sense of urgency, so I don't feel too bad about it!

I have heard mediums say that they can't switch off, and that 'spirit' is always butting in, demanding their attention. Well, I feel sorry for those people, because it would annoy the hell out of me! I wouldn't be happy if 'living' strangers continuously showed up in my home, or followed me around everywhere - I'd definitely tear them a new one, *and* phone the police! When I first started working in an intuitive capacity, and was travelling out to work with groups, some people would try to befriend me, calling me on the phone for 'a little chat'... which always led to them wanting to make use of my skills. I didn't *need* new friends - I had, and still do, more people in my life than I could manage to stay in regular contact with (as is true for many for us, with our busy lives). I found them to be intrusive, and made it clear that I have a life outside of intuitive work - that it isn't something that possesses me, 24 hours a day. I will help where and when I am able to, and if necessary; *however*, regardless of whether it is the living or the dead, there have to be boundaries!

Chapter 8

Are they connecting with *you?*

S o, I have talked about some of the ways in which non-physical souls and entities have connected with *me*, but what about you? I am, periodically, contacted by people who believe that a deceased relative is attempting to communicate with them, usually because they have had a strange dream, or they feel that they are not alone, or odd things are occurring around their home. I have come to recognise that, generally speaking, amongst these cases there is often a connection with underlying depression or anxiety. Not in every case, of course - but the numbers tend to be high. I am not going to attempt any kind of explanation for this, or offer up any guesses; I am merely reporting it as an interesting fact.

Anyway, I recently received the following message:

"I need your expertise! I have been woken a few nights in the last 6 months with a sharp double poke in my back or side, whilst I am asleep. I feel that this may be my departed dad trying to communicate for some reason, as I sleep alone."

As I said earlier, I cannot respond to every request for advice or help, but I put this lady on my list and gave a brief reply a few days later:

"Hi, I feel that whoever is poking you is responding to something that is going on within your mind and your thoughts… as if you are dithering about something, or churning it over, without looking for a way to resolve it. It feels more like a prompt for action, than anything else. When you are going to sleep, certain things keep popping up in your mind, and there is an ongoing sense of 'sameness' with you that has little to do with the current coronavirus situation. I feel that there is something on your mind that you would ideally like to bring to the fore, but are not doing so for one reason or another. Therefore, it seems that this poke is an attempt to encourage you to really think about a situation or set of circumstances that you are sitting on, and ask yourself how much longer you feel that you can continue. The next two to three months would be a

*good time to start setting certain changes in motion - and that's my brief
interpretation and analysis!"*

And I received this response:

*"Thank you so much, Leanne. There **is** something, and I **have**
been procrastinating. Xxx"*

I arrived at my conclusion by 'tuning in', and I think that
maybe it *was* her father who was doing the poking. I certainly
gained a strong sense of a down-to-earth, well-meaning male.
I suppose the reason that night-time is often favoured by non-
physical souls who wish to get our attention is that it is the
time of day when our conscious mind is less likely to be on
guard duty (that period between sleep and wake). Of course,
not all metaphysical activity takes place at night, but it
certainly isn't uncommon for it to do so.

Dreams are another way in which people feel that they
have been contacted by a deceased loved one. It is difficult to
know for sure, as dreams are often such complex and
confusing experiences; however, we have all had those
dreams that are so *real* they stay with us for days... the quality
is somehow different to the usual weird meanderings and

outpourings of our subconscious mind! The essence of the loved one remains with us, as if we have been in their actual, physical presence - and I believe that, when it feels this way to us, we *have* connected with them. I remember dreaming about my niece, and she was being rather impatient with me. I said something like, "oh my God, you are alive, you are still here!", and she retorted, "of *course* I'm still here... what are you going on about ?" When I awoke, I cried. It was as if I *had* been in her presence, but, in the cold light of day, she was still 'dead'. It seems cruel, I know, like a mean joke. I got it, though; I understood that she was trying, in her usual cheeky way, to say, "I might be gone... but I'm not GONE!" Our loved ones would never want to frighten or upset us, but even the dead feel the need to deliver a bit of straight-talking every now and then!

Sometimes we might struggle to remember the exact details of the dream - which can be really disappointing - but at least the *sense* of that person stays with us (if only for a short while). The dream may be short, or we might receive only a brief, fleeting image of the face of one who has passed, or hear a soft whisper in a voice that we recognise: it doesn't make any difference, as far as I am concerned; if it feels real to us, then it *is* real. If you feel downhearted and discouraged because you believe that you have never experienced any of the above, don't despair. I bet for sure that you will have had at least one day when the sadness of loss lifted, replaced by an inexplicable sense of connection, as if your loved one was close. When this happens, it could be that you *did* meet up in a dream, but it faded from your conscious mind as soon as you awakened (whilst being fully retained by your unconscious mind), or it could be that on that particular day, at that particular time, you were more naturally receptive to the energetic love being sent your way by a dearly missed, beloved soul. It isn't something that you can control, and it isn't something that is done the 'right' way or the 'wrong' way. We do need to remember just how technically impossible all of this should be! We are, after all, communicating *vibrationally*, mind to mind and heart to heart - and the communication has to penetrate an ever-shifting, ever-changing wall of interference. When you think about it, even the briefest of connections is a miracle… it's just that we naturally long and yearn for more.

There will be many little moments that at first lift your spirits, only to bring them crashing down again as you convince yourself that you merely imagined the thing that you so want to be real: the the brief but familiar touch to your cheek, hand, or arm; the smell of toast or coffee, when you have made neither; inexplicable but comforting little sounds of movement around the house; a special and meaningful song suddenly playing on the radio, just as a memory of a lost loved one fills your mind. These, and other similar happenings, can be so easily missed, and so easily dismissed by well-meaning doubters who don't want you to 'dwell' on such things... for your own good. Of course, nothing can ever take away the pain and emptiness of loss, but sometimes, just to get us through another day, all we need is a tiny piece of evidence that our loved one is still within reach.

However, there is a 'but' coming, and it is this: we need to make sure that we don't end up losing our way, becoming so caught up and overwhelmed that it becomes increasingly difficult for us to function in a rational way. Around 20 years ago, a middle-aged woman consulted me, convinced that she was being haunted by a specific man. I can't remember all of the details, but I think I unwittingly encouraged her... which turned out to be an unwise move. She appeared to be a smart, down-to-earth lady, and when she asked me to visit her home, as she felt that there was something energetically untoward going on there, I wasn't too concerned. To cut a long story short, I came to realise that she was neurotically obsessed with the idea of paranormal activity, constantly on the look-out for 'proof'; her husband, who had been diagnosed with cancer, appeared to be wearily resigned to the way things were... as if he'd given up trying to reason with her. Well, almost, anyway. They argued in front of me, and she furiously pointed at a space on the wall, shouting, "well, what about that picture? You know as well as I do that it suddenly fell off and hit the floor, when neither of us were anywhere near it!" His exasperation was palpable. "The string holding it onto the nail was 20 years old... it just snapped!" he told her, probably for the tenth time. She was adamant that it had been the work of a dark force, and I recognised that she was probably experiencing mental health problems, having some kind of breakdown, initiated, I imagine, by the stress of her husband's illness. I worried because I feared that I had opened up Pandora's box by listening to her tale and therefore giving it credence. I don't know how it all ended because I had no choice other than to distance myself from the situation; I was out of my depth and had no idea how to help them. However, it was an important lesson that I definitely needed to learn, and I became much more careful about how I responded to calls for help with hauntings and paranormal activity. I have long since advised people to be open to a rational, practical explanation for strange happenings *before* jumping to the conclusion that dark forces are at play. Sometimes there genuinely *is* a situation that requires the services of a paranormal investigator... but often there isn't. I feel that it is important for me to differentiate between feeling the presence of a loved one, or even an unknown but unthreatening energy, and fearing that an invisible, malicious force is infiltrating our mind and our home. My advice is, if you feel that there is some form of paranormal activity going on around you, but it isn't causing any obvious issues, leave it alone. You are merely sharing the same space! If, however, you are convinced that there is something going on that is causing you and your family to feel uncomfortable, and you *have* looked for and failed to find a rational explanation, then you should seek out the services of a professional. Rest assured that your 'dead' family and friends would never dream of haunting you... they're far too nice (and busy) for that!

Chapter 9

Mediums

Mediums work in different ways, a fact that doesn't always appear to be understood. Some are strongly clairvoyant, which means that they work visually. Others are more geared toward clairaudience, which means that they listen and hear - and *all* mediums use clairsentience to one degree or another (interpreting through sense and feeling). Mediums are human, just like everyone else, and they can have good days and not so good days; a spiritual communication consultation is a three-way process, between the medium, the customer, and the communicator, and sometimes the energetic channels are not as clean and free-flowing as we'd ideally prefer. If the customer is intent on 'testing' the medium, or is being deliberately resistant, they cannot expect the process to work as well as it potentially could. It certainly isn't pleasant for a medium to be working under those conditions. I once visited a house in which the customer's living room walls were blank - apart from a large number of picture hooks. I asked what had happened to her pictures and she told me that she'd removed them all before I arrived, to make sure that I didn't pick up any 'clues'. At least she was honest. Another group of women had made an agreement amongst themselves to tell me absolutely nothing and to answer no questions (I know, because one of them gleefully admitted to it). It was a hard evening, in what felt like an unwelcoming, hostile environment, and when I left I was so miserable and exhausted that I seriously considered quitting the work for good. I didn't, but it was experiences like this that ultimately led me to retire from travelling out and working with groups.

I understand that most people simply don't know what they are supposed to say or *not* say, when having a consultation; they don't want to do the medium's job for them, but, on the other hand, being so tight-lipped that it almost impossible to breathe is possibly taking it too far the other way! If the medium has a good reputation then it is best to relax and trust them. Some prefer to have no advance information whatsoever, others ask for certain details before they begin. If you tend to not want to supply any info at all, then you should check with the medium in advance as to whether or not they work that way, before making a booking. Remember, the purpose of a spiritual communication consultation is to (hopefully) make an energetic link with a deceased loved one; it isn't a straightforward, practical process, and I would describe it as a bit of an inexact science. I have heard mediums say that they have no control over who 'comes through', and that 'spirit' chooses the connections. Well, I am sure that that is true for *them*, but it was never something I myself subscribed to. As previously mentioned, I would always ask for the first name and age of the person who had passed, and make what I called a 'cosmic phone call'... a request for a connection with that particular soul. More often than not others would join in too, but at least I had a starting point. There is no right way or wrong way; it's just horses for courses, as they say. It isn't a competition or a test (or at least it shouldn't be); it is a process that will either deliver a little or a lot: either way, we should consider ourselves blessed.

Some very interesting questions have been raised over the years. A grieving woman once consulted me, wanting to hear from her adult son who had passed suddenly and unexpectedly. We made the link and I also explained to her that he 'felt' okay to me, that he was accepting of his situation and therefore 'at peace'. She strongly disputed that that could be true. "How can he be okay and accepting when he has left a wife and young children behind?" she demanded. I thought about it for a few seconds, and then asked her, "so, how would you feel if I told you that he is unhappy and grieving, bereft at having left his life and his loved ones behind?" This time *she* thought about it, and then sighed, deeply. "I wouldn't like it at all", she admitted. "But it's *really* hard to come to terms with. I just don't know what to think, right now."

And I understood her dilemma. It got me thinking about the divide between the one who leaves and the ones who remain. I liked this lady, she was straightforward and stoic, and I knew that she wasn't trying to be difficult; it was just too painful to face, either way, especially at that early stage of loss. I received an email from her some weeks later, thanking me and explaining that the consultation had really helped her and her family... she'd just needed some time to process it all. But I'd recognised something else, something that is common amongst the bereaved: anger. She was angry with him for leaving, she was angry with him for being 'happy', when *they* were all in such pain. It might not have been conscious anger, but it was there, nevertheless. I have worked with those whose loved ones have taken their own lives, and the anger is palpable. "How could they do this to me/us? How could they leave me to deal with all of this on my own? Why didn't they come to me? Why couldn't I help them? Why couldn't anybody have helped *us*?" It isn't wrong to be angry when someone we love, someone whose life has been very much tied up with our own, is suddenly gone. Grief can be impossible to bear, and so anger steps in until we are able to face and process it. My youngest daughter recently sobbed that she was feeling angry with her beloved cat for abandoning her the previous year. They'd been best buddies for 17 years, but Tarrant had finally succumbed to cancer, after putting up a brave fight. We have other cats, who are all dearly loved, but Tarrant was different and the relationship between her and my daughter was, without doubt, a special one. She felt that Tarrant was slipping away from her and she was struggling to feel her presence, which caused the raw grief to re-emerge, and the sense of loss to become even more acute. However, I couldn't help but believe otherwise; I just knew that the almost human cat was never going to drift away without a backward glance... that somehow she would make sure that her beloved owner received something that would fill the void and bring comfort... and, as I type this, I think that maybe that process is starting to unfold. We'll just have to wait and see.

So, how do our deceased loved ones respond to our pain and anger? To be perfectly honest, I can't say for sure. I can see why it makes no sense to us 'living' souls that they would just die and be completely happy about it... but I don't believe that it's that simple. Although we don't lose our sense of self upon passing, it seems that we do gain a more expanded understanding of the process of life and physical death. We are no longer viewing existence through the human filter. And also, it appears to me that time as we know it, here, in the physical world, is not something that exists in a non-physical dimension, or at least it behaves in a very different way. Time often feels as if it is passing very slowly here, on planet Earth, but I don't think that it is experienced that way in a non-physical dimension. This is merely my own conclusion, of course, and not something I can definitively prove. But, it would explain the different ways in which the living and the deceased respond to death... maybe. I have received communications that suggest that the one who died was a bit shocked when it happened, and some who have said that death had to creep up on them in order to 'catch them'...

but never in a maudlin, regretful way. And, I have sensed from some now-deceased souls that they wish that they'd done more with their life when they had the opportunity. That shouldn't really come as any surprise, though - after all, how many of us feel that way *now*, and when looking back? The trick is to get as much juice out of life as possible, before finally popping our earthly clogs!

Anyway, back to how the 'dead' connect with us through mediums. In my fiction book, Daniel Beyond Death, Daniel has an appointment to chat with his mum through a very nice lady; however, as it is his first experience he won't be alone - because, as Grandad Bill dryly informs him, "muggins here has been roped in as well". Daniel is fascinated by the fact that the medium can see him in his red football shirt, and smell his favourite aftershave (even though he hasn't even developed stubble), and that she knows he likes Italian food. He found that she didn't get everything exactly right, and that some stuff was a bit jumbled, but on the whole he was impressed... and delighted to have been able to see and 'talk' to his beloved mum. Spiritual communication is an energetic, emotional, mind-to-mind process; it is almost like working with radio waves, tuning in to find the clearest station. If a medium is unable to make a link with a particular deceased loved one, it doesn't mean that they aren't around or available; it just means that he or she hasn't been able to get onto the right wavelength on that occasion... and they shouldn't be castigated for it, or compared to others who were 'able to make the connection'. Every little nugget we receive should be treated like gold dust, rather than being dismissed, or deemed inadequate. After all, we *are* communicating with 'dead' people - and if *you* have been frustrated when a link wasn't as good as you'd hoped, imagine how disappointed *they* felt, knowing that you went away unhappy. It isn't all one-way traffic!

The following is an excerpt from Daniel Beyond Death, which explains the process from the 'other side', in a lighthearted way:

"Your mother will be here in a moment, she's just parking the car."

Grandad Bill was trying to appear casual, as if he was just waiting for a bus or something... but Daniel could feel the tension, and the older man was standing very close to him.

"Where are we, and who's she?" Daniel whispered. They were gazing into a small room, in which a woman, around the same age as his mum, and with shoulder length brown hair, was seated at a table. There was an empty chair opposite, and the woman seemed to be… waiting. Her hands were resting in her lap, and her eyes were closed. It wasn't totally clear though, and Daniel wondered if the room was smokey, because he was struggling to see properly. He *could* see, but it was as if he was looking through a dusty lens, and it was frustrating.

"That's Julia, she's the one your mum has come to see. She's a… oh, here's your mum now."

A man appeared at the door, holding it open for someone who squeezed past him.

The man spoke, but his words didn't register with Daniel.

"*Mum!*" He half yelled and half sobbed at the same time, and he felt Grandad Bill's presence, a bit like the Kev hug, only better. He couldn't believe what he was seeing. He knew it was his mum… he could feel her, with every inch of his being, but she didn't look the same. She was thinner, paler, and she looked older than he remembered. Even through the haze, he could see that she was a shadow of the woman she used to be. It made him feel so sad… angry even.

"I shouldn't have died! It's my fault."

"Now, now lad, keep it together. You're going to need all of your energy, but it'll be worth it in the end."

The older man had been prepared for this, and he was going to help the boy get through his first 'communication'. It was always the trickiest, especially if the wires got crossed, and the link muddled up.

Julia was speaking. "Hello Anne, please sit down."

The already tearful woman, clutching a packet of tissues, slid into the chair, and took a gulp of air.

"Thank you," she whispered.

"I can see that this is very difficult for you," Julia soothed, "but please don't worry. Obviously you are here because you want to make contact with someone who has passed, and I will do the best I can. Sometimes the link is strong, sometimes it isn't. And, if I don't make immediate contact with the person you are hoping to hear from, it won't be because they aren't available, or don't want to talk with you... it will be because I haven't been able to pick up their frequency. Do you understand?"

Anne Jackson sighed softly, and blinked. "Yes... I do. But I hope... I hope that..."

"I know, I know," the medium reached across and patted her hand. "I will do my best."

Julia closed her eyes, and breathed deeply. Daniel experienced a sudden jolt, as if a flash of lightning ran through him... and the haze started to lift. The room became clearer, and he could see the blue of the walls, the gold of the carpet, the fine grey streaks in his mother's hair… and she was wearing his black and red sweatshirt… the one he'd only worn a couple of times before… well, you know…*before*. It cheered him up, though, and made him feel close to her. He noticed that it still had a little stain on the front, where he'd dropped a tomato sauce covered chip. She'd obviously picked the top up off his bedroom floor, and put it on without washing it. Not like her… normally she'd have had it off his back and straight into the washing machine!

Grandad Bill elbowed Daniel in the ribs, grinning… doing that mind reading thing again. Julia opened her eyes and began to speak.

"I feel the presence of a young man… and my chest and my head hurt…" She winced a little. "Of course he isn't feeling that pain now, it is only a way of identifying him. He is wearing a red top… a sports type top…"

"That's my son!" Anne Jackson gasped. "He… he was hit by a car… and that's his favourite football top you can see him wearing." Her voice was swallowed by a sob, as she pressed a crumpled tissue against her lips.

Daniel looked down at himself; "I'm wearing my footie top? Oh yeah, so I am… nice one!"

"Is he okay... is he with anyone?" Anne asked, voice quivering.

"Well, of course he's fine," Julia murmured. "Let me see. He appears to be with an older man... broad, silvery grey hair, a ruddy face... your father? He had a big pain in his chest, not long before he passed." Bill nudged Daniel again, and winked. "I'm up," he said.

"Yes... yes, that sounds like my dad! Thank goodness... I'm so glad Daniel's not alone!"

"Oh, he'd never be alone," Julia laughed. "And when people die, they are more alive than we are... they are *freer*, because they are operating within a much higher vibrational dimension than this one!"

The medium closed her eyes again, and Daniel felt the shift in energy. He found himself kind of talking... but without words. He thought about his beloved Hugo Boss aftershave... not that he shaved... and lasagne... his absolute fave food... and spending hours in the shower, playing his music, full blast.

Julia touched on all of these. She told Anne she could smell an expensive perfume... a man's perfume. And she could 'taste' Italian food... and she could hear loud music and singing. Maybe she couldn't hear him totally clearly, Daniel thought, but she certainly got the gist of what he was thinking.

And Anne recognised everything. Daniel was starting to really get into it, now.

"He's showing me something heart-shaped… it looks like a little pendant… silver coloured…"

Anne nodded. "I put it in the coffin with him. He'd given it to me the Christmas before… before he died. He took my heart with him, so it seemed to be the right thing to do. Can you tell him I love him… we all love him… and we will miss him forever?"

"You just told him yourself!" Julia laughed. "And anyway, he already knew. So, what's this now?"

She closed her eyes again, and appeared to be really concentrating.

"Ah… he's rubbing the top of your head… and he says "See ya later, Annie!"

Anne Jackson actually laughed out loud. "Oh my God! He often did that on his way out of the door! He would pass my chair and ruffle up my hair, because he knew it bugged me, and he'd say, 'See ya later, Annie'… and I would say MOTHER to you, you cheeky little bugger!"

Bill could feel his grandson's relief… *and* his daughter's. Okay, the grief would never leave her until she herself made the transition, but for now she was smiling… for now she believed, wholeheartedly, that her son still existed, and that she would see him again one day. She was reassured that he wasn't lost and alone. Tonight, she would sleep a little better, though the tears would still slip between her flickering eyelids, slide down her cheeks and dampen her pillow, as she dreamed. One step at a time… one day at a time…there was no other way of doing it.

Anne Jackson wiped her eyes, took a deep breath, and sat up straight.

"Thank you, Julia. You have no idea what this means to me. And please, tell my dad and mum that we love and miss them too… and thank them for looking after Daniel."

***

Afterthought: I only remembered this little story yesterday, and I have been trying to figure out where I could fit in… without success. So, I have decided to plonk it here, at the end of this chapter!

I once conducted a consultation in which I made a link with two young men from the same family; sadly, they had both died in (separate) car accidents. One of them suddenly held up what appeared to be a narrow board, upon which was displayed two words, in neon letters… a first name and a surname. I read them out loud, and my customer said, "it's the name of the boy you have been describing to me - he's my son!" I can promise you, I had absolutely no prior knowledge that would allow me to create a hoax message and I was absolutely thrilled! How *clever* of him! It isn't something that I have ever experienced with any other communicator. All I can say is, that lad's got a great future ahead of him!.

Chapter 10

Spirit guides

Warning! Incoming rant - I just remembered something that made me really cross!

Some years ago, I received a phone call from a lady who was incredibly upset (I will call her Mary); she wanted to ask my advice over something that had happened the previous evening. She had attended her weekly spiritual development class, whereupon they had entered into a meditation under the guidance of the woman who ran the group. The purpose was to connect with their spirit guides, and Mary was delighted to find herself engaging with a native American Indian chief, adorned in full headdress. After the meditation was complete, she couldn't wait to tell the lady in charge (I will call her Val) all about her experience. However, Val immediately rose up, firmly informing her that, "you have to tell him to back off, immediately! You aren't ready for that kind of connection yet!", and Mary was devastated. She was disappointed, confused, and looking for reassurance. I, on the other hand, was extremely peed off. "Tell Val to mind her own business!" I asserted. "How the hell does she know what you are ready for? If it felt real to you, and it felt right and comfortable for you, then it *is* right. I am sorry that you have had this experience, but that's the trouble with *some* of these groups… ego gets in the way, and development is hindered rather than helped."

I don't know what became of the whole situation, but I do know that Mary felt a whole lot better by the end of the call. I have to admit, my cynical side tends to come to the fore where this subject is concerned, although I fully accept that that probably comes from an unfairly judgemental attitude based purely upon my own experience. I know of two spiritualist churches whose doors closed as a result of power-plays, back-biting, and infighting. I *used* to provide services for spiritualist churches, but I increasingly became uncomfortable with the way in which they were being operated, and some of the attitudes I encountered. Of course,

I am NOT suggesting that every single spiritual establishment is guilty of the same stuff (in fact, I worked with one particular church that was an absolute breath of fresh air); I am only talking about my *own* experiences and my personal interpretation of them. I found that there was also often little innovation or questioning... and those who *did* question were usually put firmly back in their place in the most patronising way. *And,* there was something *else* that completely rubbed me up the wrong way (see, I *told* you that I was going to rant!): smugness. In fact, I came up with a portmanteau: 'SPUGS' (spiritual smugs). I remember sitting at a table that was acting as an altar, alongside the man who was going to 'chair' for me, and I commented, "I love Conversations With God, book 2; everytime I have a question I can just randomly open it and I usually find an answer" (you can tell how many years ago this was). His response was, "oh, so you don't go *within* for your answers then, Leanne?" I won't repeat what I said in reply, but it shut him up. Mind you, this is the same person who, when I said that there were so many places I would love to see before I die, replied, "well you don't need to, do you? You can visit them all in the afterlife." Maybe so, my friend... but I am supposed to do *some* stuff whilst I am still *alive*!

I have been around the spiritual fraternity for long enough to know that smugness is an ever-present irritant (and some would *smugly* inform me that *they* don't allow themselves to be affected by such stuff - or worse, they'd claim never to attract it into their life in the first place because their mindset won't allow it. I have news for you: you don't attract it because you *are* it!). As I write this, we are still in lockdown due to coronavirus, and I have noticed that the spugs have upped their game on social media. Glibly informing terrified people that it is their inner and outer dialogue that is the *actual* source of their pain, and that they are more likely to leave themselves open to attracting the virus, is akin to giving them a slap in the face. I don't *entirely* disagree, but there is a way of going about things, and there is a time and a place. We aren't responsible for every last little thing that life throws our way, regardless of what the spugs would have us believe (although you could argue that we *are* responsible for the way in which we respond to those things; it just isn't always that easy, is it, to catch ourselves before we react and panic?). Life is miraculous and amazing, but it can also be unbearably cruel and unjust, at times. I suspect that some spugs struggle to deal with the negative aspects of life on planet Earth, which is why they are quick to close others down when they are struggling. Some just seem to have a superiority complex and love themselves to pieces. Either way, spiritual smugness is really about blaming, shaming, and accusing. As a young child, my primary education was provided by the kind of Catholic school that was determined to program you to accept your own sinful, worthless nature, on a daily basis (unless your parents took you to church every Sunday, in which case you were 'good'. If they didn't, you were deemed to be 'bad', and more often than not humiliated in front of your classmates on a Monday morning. And, if you foolishly lied about your attendance, it would be investigated, resulting in a stinging handprint on the back of your leg that would last for hours). There have been occasions upon which I have recognised a similarity between some people's version of spirituality, and staunch religion. Joyless, judgemental, and elitist. And all of this is relevant to the title of this book because it is highlighting how the relationship that we develop with the spirit of life itself can be negatively influenced by others. My primary school, and my paternal grandmother, presented to me a God who was, quite frankly, a nasty piece of work; controlling, domineering, unpredictable, and vengeful. I couldn't relate to *him* (we were assured that God was definitely a man). In fact, sometimes he even reminded me of my father. Luckily, I was always a questioner, and I didn't accept their story. Spirituality and religion are supposed to be about love, and the freedom to be authentic to the unique soul that we are; it is supposed to be about support, and guidance, and developing wisdom… about a connection to the source of all that is… about our own 'roots'. Well, in an ideal world, at least. I am aware that including the 'G' word in a publication is a risky thing to do; some people really don't like it. God is a dirty word to them and they respond by turning away. I am not preaching, or attempting to convert anyone. Believe what you want to believe. All I am trying to convey is that we have to be aware of how easy it is to become sucked into a set of beliefs that are not our own, and are spiritually and emotionally destructive. We have to continue to question, challenge, and reassess. That way, we get to develop our own precious relationship with the spiritual nature of life - something we can consciously nurture and protect.

There is just one last thing I want to say, before I finish this sermon! It seems fair to say that all that glitters is not gold; spirituality is not always as it is presented. Mary's joy at connecting with her spirit guide was crushed by someone who clearly wished to retain control of the group and the way in which it developed. There is nothing 'spiritual' about that, because the spirit is a free-flowing, joyful energy (as expressed in my book, Our Life Beyond Death - An Incredible Journey). Non-physical souls do not behave in this way - it is a purely human habit. Anyway, I could go on and on, but I think that this is probably an appropriate time to quit ranting and get back to the subject of spirit guides!

So, here's a question: was Mary's spirit guide *really* a native American Indian chief? Around 30/40 years ago, people often described their spirit guide as being an Indian, or a nun, or a small Chinese man (there were others, but these appeared to be the most popular). I don't know if that is still true today, as I haven't kept up to date with the subject, but I think that things have probably changed since then. As previously mentioned, 'dead' people don't have a physical body, and when I say 'dead' people I am not just talking about our family and friends. There is a network of support available from other, non-physical beings, if we are open to them - and that network probably changes as we go through different stages of life. Maybe there are one or two who consistently 'work' with us, whilst others come and go. I believe that it is probably personal to each and every one of us, and that there isn't a one-size-fits-all process. Because an energetic being does not have a physical body, it has to create an image, which is then displayed upon the screen of our mind, in order for us to 'see' it (a deceased loved one will present an image that reflects how they looked when they were fit and well, *or* as they were just before they passed… sometimes both, for extra evidence). Obviously, the energetic being, or in this case spirit guide, wants to present itself in a way that will be easily accepted and trusted by its 'student'. No good showing up as King Kong or Attila the Hun! I have no idea whether or not Mary's guide had ever *been* a native American Indian chief; it may have, in one of its physical incarnations, or it may just be that it knew that Mary would respond well to that particular image. It wanted her to feel safe and comfortable, in order for her to be open to the connection. It's pretty clever stuff, if you ask me!

I have an interesting story from my own life, about an energetic being that you might call a guide. First, however, I should explain that I no longer actually have a spirit guide, in the *accepted* sense… I just talk to someone in my head, usually addressing it as 'God', as in: "God, what do you think about this or that?" Or, "God, what do I need to do *now*, in order to sort *this* out?" Or, "Thank you God, for my good fortune, and a life that is so blessed." And yes, it does respond, in its own way, but I can't say whether it *is* God, or a spirit guide, or my own higher self (which some would say is God, anyway). It doesn't matter to me - it works, and that is all I need to know. However, I *used* to feel the need to have a spirit guide in my life (remember the one who used to like to write things down!), and there came a time when I developed a relationship with an energetic being who presented itself to me as a young, bohemian man with shoulder length brown hair... and who always appeared with his shirt unbuttoned, revealing a bare, unhairy chest! One day, I was at a friend's house and was sitting opposite to her when she suddenly said, "this might sound odd, but I can see the outline of a man standing to your left, and there is a green light pouring from him and into your chest area." I was surprised, but also relieved; I had been experiencing the most awful chest pain for days and was secretly convinced that I was going to have a heart attack. She didn't know any of this, however. I asked her to describe the 'person' she was seeing... and she told me that it was a young-looking male with long hair! I was so pleased that he was there, and even more pleased about the green light he was pouring into my heart (green is the colour of the heart chakra). As we talked, I could feel the awful pressure within my chest lessening, and within hours the pain had gone completely. I had been living an incredibly stressful life for a long time, and I realised that the emotional pain was starting to invade my body. Afterwards, I thought about how my spiritual healer appeared to look, to me - and therefore to my friend - and I realised that he reminded me of a young Jim Morrison, as portrayed in the film, Wayne's World 2! I had created that image because of the place that I was in, in my life... it represented the youthful free spirit I yearned for (plus, it was quite attractive!). And it was then that I started to understand that an energy who wants to connect with us in a loving, supportive way will allow us to unconsciously choose how it appears! I could be wrong, of course, but it seems to make sense.

Somewhere along the line I naturally gravitated away from my bohemian friend, as I evolved and headed in a different direction. That doesn't necessarily mean that our connection came to an end... it is more likely that it just changed shape and form. And, by the way, I am not suggesting that people should grow out of having spirit guides! We connect in ways that are unique to *us*, at whatever stage in life we happen to be at. Whatever works for *us*, works... it's as simple as that. Having our own dedicated guide and friend can cause us to feel supported, strong, and less alone - *because*, despite living in a world that is inhabited by at least 7 billion other souls, it is still so easy to feel the pain of spiritual and emotional loneliness. My own life would be empty, and a lot more scary, without my trusty 'voice'!

A young woman recently asked me how we actually acquire spirit guides, and all I could tell her was that we've probably always had them, but that maybe we need to give them permission to help us! I myself have been open to certain energetic beings throughout the years, but increasingly I felt that I wanted to do things on my own... a bit like a toddler whose parent quietly oversees the proceedings from the sidelines (rarely interfering, but always there in the background), looking on as she determinedly dresses and feeds herself, convinced of her own independence. The question is, how *would* we give permission to a guide to come forward and be more obviously proactive? Well, by communicating with it! If we have no awareness of a relationship with an energy that would *feel* like a guide to us, then we can quietly spend time alone, gently meditating, or simply closing our eyes and relaxing our mind, whilst issuing an 'invitation'. It might produce results immediately, or it might require several sessions; it doesn't really matter. Eventually, we will start to recognise something that becomes increasingly familiar to us... like the essence of someone we just know that we can trust. We might even catch a glimpse of an image, projected upon the screen of our mind. After that, we need to stay in touch… have a little chat every now and then, share some of our private thoughts - talk about our feelings, and our hopes and dreams. No-one else ever needs to know, if that's the way you want it. It's your guide and your business! If you feel that you won't be able to do this on your own, then there are plenty of people out there who specialise in 'spirit guide readings' (as I said earlier, always try and go on recommendation, when making a booking with any type of intuitive worker).

By the way, and just for the record, I have noticed that people often tend to be temperamentally well-matched with their guides. Some folk appear to have very grown up ones; mine have always been mischievous non-conformists! It'll be interesting for you to discover the nature of the energetic being who has elected to be one of *your* kindred spirits!

Chapter 11

Ouija boards

I was 16 years old and had just started my very first job… in the mind-numbingly boring office of a large Manchester insurance company. I was a lowly junior, fobbed off with all of the duties that no-one else could be bothered with, and paid peanuts. And then Christine joined the team.

Christine was mischievous and she led me astray; rarely a day went by without us getting into trouble for this or for that (if I hadn't landed a much nicer and better paid job, I probably would have been fired). However, one stormy, thundery day, our usually prim and proper supervisor surprised us by taking us down into the cellar beneath the big old building that housed the insurance company… to conduct a 'seance'! To be honest, I can't really remember what happened, except that it made a tedious day a lot more exciting, and it got us all stirred up. We wanted more!

That night, Christine travelled home with me on the bus to my sister's house, where I was staying until I found my own flat. We had our tea and then sat down with paper, scissors, and a pen. We cut out lots of squares upon which we wrote the letters of the alphabet and the words 'yes' and 'no'. We set up camp in the kitchen, arranging the squares in a circle on the table, with an upturned glass in the centre.

Now, before I go any further, I need to explain something; my sister's name is Kate, and on the evening in question she was hosting a tupperware party (or suchlike) for a group of friends, one of whom was called Kath. They were going to be using the living room, leaving Christine and I to our own devices in the kitchen.

So, there we were, seated at the table, each with a finger lightly resting on the upturned glass, giggling like idiots… until it started to move. Backward and forward it went, in slow jerky movements, and so we decided to ask 'it' some questions. "What is your name?" It spelled out 'Gill'. "Is there anything you want to tell us, Gill?" The glass slid across the table; "tell K come to me". Fascinated, I quickly asked, "Which K do you mean? My sister, or…", and before I'd even finished, the glass shot across the table to the square upon which was written the word 'yes'.

"It wants Kate!" I shouted, dashing into the living room, almost tripping over my own feet. "Kate, it wants *you*! Come on, hurry up!", at which point the blood drained from my sister's face, and she threw out her hands as if to ward me - or it - off. "No! I'm not coming! Tell it to go away!"

Disappointed, I returned to the kitchen and dropped into my seat. A terrified Christine was pressed up against the back door, ready to make a dash for it if anything ghostly suddenly manifested itself - but I was determined to carry on. I placed my finger just *above* the glass this time, and said, "I'm sorry, she doesn't want to talk to you. Is there anything I can help you with?" Again, before I'd even finished speaking, the glass moved swiftly across the table, and spelled out, "No, K says go away." And then, the glass touched the letter T, followed by the letter O, and moved towards L. "It's going to say 'too late', I whispered, and the glass whizzed across to the word yes. Wow. There was a weird, dense atmosphere in the little room that was almost physical, as if you could take a knife and cut a hole in it. "Okay," I said, strongly sensing that it no longer wished to carry on with the communication. "I'm sorry that we couldn't help you. Goodbye." The glass moved slowly toward the letter g and then stopped… and the pressure in the room immediately dropped, returning the air to 'normal'. I realised that I had either been holding my breath, or the density had been making it more difficult to breathe. I was also struck by the sense of sadness that had accompanied 'Gill's' words, as she (?) explained that it was too late (although misspelled); Kate had said *no* to her, and that was the end of it. My sister was not impressed, and in hindsight, I can understand why! She had no memory of ever knowing anyone named Gill, and we never did find out who she/he/it was, or what they wanted from Kate.

But, I can tell you one thing; Christine and I almost scared ourselves to death! She was so afraid that I had to travel with her on her bus for home, and then make my way back… on my own. For days, I was sure that something shadowy was following me, and every little sound and movement made me jump. However, the worst thing was the dream. I had been sleeping with my bedroom door open, and one night I fell into an unsettled sleep, still a little disturbed and anxious. As I drifted off, I found myself watching a man as he climbed the stairs - and then all of a sudden he was right in *front* of me, laughing wickedly, as if he found it highly amusing to terrify me! I shot up in bed, heart pounding, stifling a scream. And that was the last time I dabbled with the ouija (well, almost the last time). But here's an interesting little fact: remember the dark-skinned guy who cheekily raised a glass to me in the pub, giving me a shiver and causing me to disconnect? It was the same man! I recognised him instantly, even though I hadn't thought about the ouija incident for years. It seems that he had been keeping an eye on me... *possibly* for my own good! I have to laugh when I remember what he was wearing as he climbed the stairs: a sheepskin coat, with the collar turned up. He reminded me of a used-car salesman! I don't know... he *was* scary, but there was also a dark kind of humour about him. So, as I say, maybe his job has been to keep me in line. Or maybe not...

Anyway, fast-forward a couple of years to a time when I was living in a tiny flat with a shared bathroom. I had invited a group of friends over from work, and much alcohol was consumed... leading us to decide that we'd have a dabble with the ouija (you'd think I would know better, wouldn't you?).

Once again, paper, pen, and scissors were rooted out, and we squashed around a coffee table, trying to be serious… which proved to be almost impossible! Then, the only other girl in the group, Beverley, announced that she was desperate to use the loo. However, the woman with whom I shared the bathroom had a habit of hogging it whenever I had visitors (which wasn't that often), and Beverley couldn't wait for Blanche to finish whatever it was she was doing, and so headed outside to find a convenient bush. Minutes later she returned, informing us that she'd gone into the field next door and relieved herself behind a rock. When I explained that the 'field' was actually an old cemetery, and that the 'rock' was probably a gravestone, she thought that I was kidding (I wasn't) and wouldn't believe me. Anyway, we settled down, determined to take contacting the dead more seriously… and we *almost* managed it, until one of the boys put on a creepy voice, and in a loud whisper said, "Beverleeee…. You p****d on my grave. I am going to get you for that!" We fell about laughing, and gave it up as a bad job. Utterly disrespectful, I know - but we *were* young and rather drunk. And, in all honesty, I was lucky that it ended that way, otherwise I might have had another 'visit'!

You have just read two completely different stories about the experience of using ouija - and I suspect that most people who have dabbled will report having been in either the first or the second group! I wouldn't use a ouija board nowadays, simply because there wouldn't be any point in doing so; I have no need for it, and any entertainment value it might have held was left behind with my youthhood. However, I am not going to offer dire warnings about bad luck, disaster, or even death. If people want to involve themselves with the ouija they should do so with their eyes wide open and their feet on the ground. And, they should also be clear with themselves about what it is they are hoping to achieve. More often than not the attraction *is* entertainment..., but, as I explained in the chapter about ghost hunting, in my book, Our Life Beyond Death - be careful what you wish for... you just might get it! Being scared to within an inch of our lives by the unknown can be a seductive idea... until we are! I believe that some people *have* connected with a deceased relative through a ouija board (or at least they strongly believe that they have), but this is not the usual or recommended way of going about spiritual communication. I have no doubt in my mind that whoever Gill was, a genuine connection was made that day... but it definitely wasn't a happy one. The energy that came with it was heavy and sad. I am not an expert on the subject of ouija, and so I can only share my own personal experiences, thoughts, and feelings. I certainly wouldn't actively encourage anyone to become too involved with it, though I do believe that a good percentage of what is reported by those who have used ouija should be taken with a pinch of salt, or at least intelligently investigated. Imagination and fear can be a pretty powerful combination! If there is even a tiny possibility that lost and unhappy souls could latch onto us through the use of something that we don't really understand, *would* we choose to expose ourselves to it?

So, yes, the ouija board *is* a means through which the 'dead' can connect with us - and vice versa. But, it remains an unknown quantity (as far as I'm concerned, anyway). If you are still open to exploring it further, my advice would be to do your research and consult with someone who has seriously studied and practised it, and has earned a respectable reputation. I don't believe that it should be seen as a parlour game; you just never know what you might leave yourself open to. And yes, I have said that we can always disconnect from an energy that is becoming uncomfortable or intrusive, but why take the chance when there are other, maybe more tried and tested, ways of making a link with non-physical souls?

Chapter 12

A recording on the face of time...

I carefully climbed the old creaking stairs, hoping that they wouldn't give way beneath me. I shouldn't have been there, of course; even though the crumbling house appeared to be abandoned, I was, to all intents and purposes, trespassing. It was just that the place intrigued me, sitting up there on a hill, quietly rotting away. It had clearly been an attractive-looking building at one time, and I was keen to discover what it looked like on the inside.... which, as it turned out, was a mess. I didn't go any further than the top step, as the bedroom walls were down and I could see several holes in the floor. Suddenly, a scene unfolded in my mind, and I watched as a dapper-looking man fastened his jacket buttons and placed a cap on his head, whilst a woman, still in her dressing gown, bustled around him. And then it faded. I assumed that these people had passed, but were occupying a version of the house that no longer existed in this world. I was wrong.

Later that day, I told our nearest neighbours about my little adventure, and what I had seen. Their family had lived there for generations, and they seemed to know everything about everyone. They told me that the couple I described had indeed lived in the now decrepit house... *and* that they were alive and well, and living in a nearby village! He was always immaculately presented, and his wife rarely got dressed before lunchtime. They were not 'ghosts' - they were imprints on the face of time! What I had tapped into was a recording of a tiny part of their life... and not even a very exciting one! However, that recording revealed a lot about them and how they lived, the energy of which became embedded within the walls of what used to be their home. Amazing!

It wasn't a massive revelation to me that this could happen; after all, we all know that 'energy' is a potent force which can definitely be experienced - usually as an atmosphere, or an inexplicable feeling or sense. Wherever we go, we leave something of ourselves behind, like an airplane trail; if we are just passing through it will fade, but if we occupy a space for long enough, we could leave an impression that might never fully dissipate. Strong emotions tend to make the most significant dent, especially if they have been experienced over an elongated time period. However, consistent habits will also leave their mark. Generally speaking, most of us remain largely oblivious to the energetic recordings, though some people are more naturally sensitive to them than others. Emotionally charged echoes of the past *can* become problematic, and can even be 'fed' by the present. There have been several occasions on which I have been consulted over unsettling paranormal activity, and have suspected that the disturbance is *probably* being unconsciously and unwittingly created by at least one of the occupants. Long term anger and depression can definitely play a role, but here's a thought: what if an emotionally vulnerable individual moves into a property that is already embedded with the negative energy of past residents? For all of us, there *could* be a valid argument in favour of carrying out a background check, *and* some kind of energetic clearing, before moving into any home that is new to *us*! Some sneer at the idea of buying clothes from charity (thrift) shops because they don't like the idea of wearing something that was previously worn by a stranger. I ask those people if they have ever moved house. If the answer is yes, the next question has to be, "have you ever taken up residence in a house that was occupied by other people *before* you?" Mostly, it's an affirmative. Well, there isn't much difference, to be honest! I personally have no issue with charity shop gear - I have come across some fantastic bargains! - but I can see why some people aren't comfortable with the idea. It just comes down to individual choice. However, if you think about it, wrapping ourselves - our entire family, even - in someone else's residual energy, is maybe even worse than wrapping ourselves in their old clothes! Just saying...

Anyway, before we go any further, I should make it clear that I am not claiming to be an expert on the subject of hauntings versus energetic recordings; there are people out there who genuinely understand a considerable amount more about it than I do. Also, I am not suggesting that every single case of paranormal disturbance is the result of emotional overload. I am just explaining that, sometimes, it *is*... and that what we might fear is the work of a malicious, non-physical being, could actually be more connected to *this* world. It isn't always easy to figure out, but it makes sense to be open to all possibilities.

I have just recalled a fascinating example of what I believed to be a destructive recording of the past, rather than a haunting. It occurred in a house I was invited to, to provide individual consultations for a small group of people. As so often happened, I was informed that 'something' was causing problems for the family, especially the husband. He had taken to sleeping in the guest room, so as not to disturb his wife, and was becoming increasingly depressed. Convinced that there was a negative energy in that room (the lady of the house assured me that even the dog wouldn't go in there), he had abandoned it in favour of the couch. I agreed to take a look, and, as is always the way with animals and children, the dog made a liar of the woman by trotting in as if it didn't have a care in the world! Nevertheless, I sat for a while, opening my mind to the energy of what was a cosy and nicely presented little room… until it changed. Suddenly, I was in a cold and miserable space, made up of what appeared to be bare stone walls and a concrete floor. The light was dull, and there was no furniture, apart from a wooden rocking chair… which suddenly began to move backward and forward in a frantic manner, as if propelled by an incredibly disturbed occupant. As bad as that looked and felt, it got worse when what I can only describe as a ball of energy started to furiously bounce from one wall to another. The general atmosphere of the room was one of utter misery and despair. Although I have no proof, I remain convinced that some poor soul, probably suffering from either a physical or a mental health problem, had been held prisoner in that room - hidden away from the world - possibly for years on end. No wonder the poor guy felt worse after sleeping in there, given that he was already struggling to cope with life. Looking back, I don't believe that a now-deceased soul was haunting the room; I think that it's far more likely that what was trapped within those walls was an awful echo of the past... a heartbreaking memory. A lot of people would have remained oblivious. However, it took just one temporarily vulnerable soul to draw attention to it - and once that 'door' was opened, it wasn't going to be easily closed. I gave them the phone number of a friend who has worked with this kind of situation in the past, often with positive results, and wished them the very best of luck. The couple *were* having relationship problems, which in turn were hurting the family; however, I felt that there was definitely a lot of love there and that they *would* make it through (with a bit outside help, and some ongoing communication). However, first and foremost, that 'ghost' of the past really needed to be healed, allowing new, fresh energy to be released into what could be a very happy family home.

If you think about it, many, many establishments boast a resident 'spirit' who wanders the corridors and staircases, late at night. It can be a powerful selling point! However, is the 'grey lady', who can often be spotted drifting across the top landing at midnight, *really* treading the same old bit of carpet, again and again? And, if so, for how long? Eternity? That seems a bit harsh. Better to imagine that she is just an energetic tape recording from days gone by, running on a loop! I have no idea why some moments that are captured in time remain so visible. Maybe by paying attention to them we are keeping them alive... recharging the batteries, so to speak!.

Chapter 13

Hopes, fears, and doubts

In this final chapter I am going to repeat a little of what I have already said (never hurts to be reminded!), because it is relevant to a couple of additional insights I would like to leave you with!

Grieving people often tell me that they want to develop their own mediumistic skills in order to be able to connect with their lost loved ones. And I can absolutely understand why. However, it often doesn't end up working out that way, mostly because of doubt. Even if we develop our skills to a degree that allows us to work on behalf of others, when it comes to making a link with someone *we* love and miss, it is difficult for us to be sure that we aren't imagining whatever we see or feel, because we want it so badly. I don't have an answer for that, I am afraid. It may not be true for everyone, of course, but it certainly is for the many disappointed hopefuls who have approached me for advice. I have come to the conclusion that maybe our motivation for wanting to work in a mediumistic capacity shouldn't be to help ourselves… and I don't mean that in a judgemental way. I am not suggesting that it is selfish and wrong, and that intuitive ability is a 'gift' that should only be used for the benefit of others. I am explaining that it appears to me that we are more likely to be able to make periodic links with our own deceased loved ones when we have become an *accomplished* medium, which, generally speaking, requires time and experience. And even then an element of doubt is usually still present. This does not take anything away from what I have already said about natural, spontaneous connections with our loved ones; here, I am talking about the desire to communicate with them in the same way that a medium would. I am not dismissing the idea, and I would never discourage anyone who wishes to develop their intuitive ability in order to attempt to open up communication channels with their own beloved family and friends. We should be open to all possibilities, whilst being consciously aware of the potential pitfalls and difficulties.

As previously discussed, fear is something that strikes virtually everyone who enters into the initial exploration of the world of spiritual communication. Fear of attracting a 'dark energy', fear of becoming overwhelmed, fear of being seen as crazy or delusional, fear of the unknown... and *none* of these fears are unreasonable. We *should* be aware. But, as I have said, we always have the ability to disconnect whenever we need to (although, in my experience, some convince themselves that they can't, because they don't feel strong enough. It is never true, but it may be that they would benefit from a little help from an appropriate outside source. Very occasionally, however, an individual will say that they want to disconnect... whilst continuing to go back for more). Our own loved ones and our guiding energies would never want to hurt or scare us. However, if we are serious about becoming more accomplished at opening up channels of communication, we need to be willing to have a variety of experiences. We can't recognise and embrace the light without accepting the existence of the dark - something we need to become healthily respectful of!

There is another fear that I haven't yet mentioned: the fear of mediums! Look, let's not pretend that everyone who works within the spiritual/psychic arena is spiritually healthy and above reproach - or even sane. It is an industry that has traditionally attracted - how shall we say it… more than its fair share of less than grounded individuals? Which is one of the reasons it has had to battle such a bad reputation. In my role as an intuitive consultant, I have worked with many women who have lied to their partners about their whereabouts, in order to avoid a row… or even being prevented from attending. People 'like me' are seen as con-artists and rip-off merchants who make a living by 'preying on the vulnerable'… in certain quarters, at least. Which is why there are customers who voluntarily attend an appointment, whilst responding to the consultant/reader in a hostile, distrusting way. They *want* to use the service, but at the same time they are terrified of being fooled and lied to. *Especially* where spiritual communication is concerned. It's a risk, isn't it, particularly if the medium isn't one with whom they are familiar. I always advise, where possible, to rely upon recommendation when seeking out the services of an intuitive consultant, be it for mediumship or prediction and insight. One of my own fears has been of being lumped in with all of the dodgy characters who are, far too often, held up as an accurate representation of the psychic and spiritual world - a fear that has been realised *many* times (and, despite which, I lived to tell the tale!). However, my biggest fear has always been of not being good enough as a medium. No matter what you deliver, it is never enough - you *always* wish that you could see and feel more, on behalf of the grieving and the broken hearted… *and* the 'dead' themselves. It's a big responsibility… no, a huge responsibility! However, all any of us can ever do is our best, and at least I can say, with hand on heart, that it *is* something I have always tried to do when working in an intuitive capacity. I am blessed to be able to report that there *have* been some amazing connections between myself, the customer, and those who are - how shall we say it? - now experiencing themselves and their existence in a very uplifted and expanded way!

So, there you have it; we have done what we set out to do, which was to take a look at the variety of ways in which the 'dead' connect with us - and vice versa. I would like to bring my meanderings to a close by leaving you with a little gift of two poems I wrote a very long time ago, and a sample chapter from my book, *Our Life Beyond Death* - An Incredible Journey. I hope you enjoy them, and I wish for you everything that you wish for yourself… plus a whole lot more that is good and wonderful!

Leanne Halyburton

A Journey's End

You've lost a love so dear to you, you fear you can't go on,

There once was life and warmth and hope - but now the light has gone.

I tell you from my heart, my friend, I know we do not die.

I've felt the touch of those who've gone, as gentle as a sigh.

I've caught a glimpse of smiling face, of eyes that shine with fun -

I know they're with us when we wake, and when the day is done.

From babies who were never born, to loved ones frail and old,

How blessed am I to say, "they're here!", a gift worth more than gold.

From those who sadly took their lives, to those who passed in pain -

How blessed am I to hear the words, "I'm happy, once again!"

We have to live, complete our lives, when those we love have passed.

They've gone ahead, a mile or so, but love will always last.

Be patient if you can, my friend, though grief is hard to bear:

I've seen them, so I know it's true, the ones we love are there!

Precious friends are close to you, your family's always near,

And when your journey's finally through, be proud to say, "I'm here!

"I've made mistakes, but done my best, climbed high and fallen low."

Then loving arms will welcome you - "we know, my friend, we know."

Leanne Halyburton

When I See You Again

When I see you again I will ask how you've been,

I will talk of my life and the things I have seen.

I will watch you so closely, as memories abound,

For life had less colour without you around.

I will talk of how cheated, how angry and low,

How sad we became when you left us to go.

I will detail the flowers, each kind thought and word,

But you'll smile as you murmur, "I saw and I heard.

"I was there with you all, how could I not be?

"My life celebrated, that love was for me.

"Where else would I go, with my loved ones in pain?

"I held you and kissed you, again and again.

"I'm so pleased to see you, my dearest sweet friend.

"If only you'd known that death isn't the end,

"You'd have saved yourself heartache, and tears like the sea -

"For here we are, now again, just you and me."

I will breathe in your essence, you'll touch me and say:

"It's lovely to see you - you're home now, to stay."

Our Life Beyond Death - An Incredible Journey

A medium's observations and conclusions

Quick intro!

The last thing you might expect an experienced medium to talk about is scepticism. But I *have* been sceptical, and I *have* questioned, and I *have* challenged - myself, mostly.

You see, it is so easy to become caught up in the drama, and to end up repeating and teaching the same stuff that someone else has repeated and taught to *us*… without ever asking ourselves if it actually makes sense *to us*? Over the years I came to intensely dislike the way in which spiritual communication was being presented through the media, recognising that huge pressure was being exerted upon popular 'celebrity' mediums by those who wanted to make lucrative television programs and sell lots of books. I have no problem with money being made; we live in a commercial world and the ridiculous days of expecting intuitive individuals to give their skills away for nothing have long gone (I hope).

However, things became stretched and distorted, and the 'real' message was lost - the message about how life and death fit together, and how amazing that process is; the message that reminds us that the physical life that is lived *before* death is a powerful, vital link in the chain of each soul's individual existence - and that nothing is ever lost or deemed meaningless. The focus became the medium him or herself and how 'good' they were (and some *were* and *are* incredibly good at what they do)... but it all became a bit of a galloping roadshow in which people's emotions were being manipulated and played upon in order to attract viewings. Over time, I experienced less and less desire to be a part of that, even though I gave hundreds of stage demonstrations and featured on radio. Nowadays, only a very tiny part of my business is dedicated to mediumship, but my belief in the ongoing sense of *self*, and in a continued awareness, has strengthened and grown. We are all going to die from this world one day. I don't shun the idea, dismissing it as morbid or scary, although I am in no hurry to go! And, of course, I especially don't want my loved ones to go because I would miss them with every last ounce of my being - at least, until I popped my own clogs, anyway. I don't spend my life wondering what to expect when I die - but I *do* feel that it is a subject we should all explore... one that we *should* question and challenge. I am not asking anyone to believe exactly what I believe, or to view the journey of life *after* life in the same way that I do; my truth is just that: *mine*. It might not be yours. I have a feeling that our experience beyond physical death is personal and unique to each soul... a bit like DNA. My only intention with this book is sharing: stories, perceptions, and possibilities. Even if you disagree with some or all of my ramblings, I hope you will find something that makes you smile and even raises a question or two; after all, there should always be room for an extra little bit of food for thought!

Chapter 1

A little bit of backstory!

The young man placed a bottle of red wine on the table and stepped back, smiling. I had no idea who he was but my customer recognised the description - and she understood his message completely. "He was a good friend and would often bring me a bottle of my favourite Merlot," she explained.

The young girl watched me from the corner of my kitchen. She was wearing a light coloured hoodie and chewing on her thumb, which was poking through a hole in the cuff. She 'communicated', through images in my mind, that whilst dressing her for her coffin they had struggled to put one of her shoes on. Her mother, listening to me at the other end of the telephone line, knew nothing about it. Several days later she emailed me to say that she had been in touch with the funeral home, and yes, they'd confirmed that they *had* had problems fitting one of her daughter's shoes.

The little boy showed me an image of himself walking through a doorway and I understood that he had passed very suddenly indeed: here one moment, gone the next. I was told that he'd suffered a sudden, fatal, heart failure. He kept showing me a toy vehicle whilst making "brmm brmm" noises, over and over again. My customer, his mother's friend, had attended the funeral and she explained that it was probably his favourite Ghostbusters car which had been placed on top of his coffin.

The little girl, who'd passed only hours earlier, 'showed' me the rocking horse that had been on her hospital ward... and how she would hold her nose because of the smell of her father's breath. I was a little uncomfortable delivering *that* particular message but her mother laughed, explaining that her husband loved to eat cheese and onion crisps and her daughter always hated the smell! The child also communicated that a tree was being planted in her honour, but her mother was baffled; they were still coming to terms with the loss of their daughter and hadn't thought that far ahead. The following day a friend called to let them know that they had planted a tree in her memory.

These days I no longer do much as a medium, for a number of reasons (none of them sinister!); sadly, as the years have passed by, I have forgotten many of the stories told by those who are no longer physically with us. But, the sense of being part of something greater than anything I can see with my eyes or feel with my conscious senses has grown stronger and stronger. I used to worry, to seriously question *everything*, even whilst working as a medium. I was uncomfortable with the twee, neatly packaged version of life after death that was often presented and accepted as absolute fact; so much of it didn't make any sense to me. I desperately wanted to understand what it was all *really* about and to deliver an authentic service to my customers. I wanted them to be able to really *feel* the essence of their loved ones and not just provide them with dry bits of 'evidence'. I often felt inadequate, fearing that even the best I was able to deliver wasn't good enough - and that no matter what I *was* able to receive and explain, I *always* believed it should be more!

However, I did begin to realise that very often it is the small, seemingly inconsequential things that mean so much to the grieving customer: a bottle of red wine; a shoe that wouldn't fit; a toy car; a little family joke. I have heard many people sneeringly ask, "if we can communicate with the dead, how come they never tell us anything important or earth-shattering?"

Well, I don't think it's their job to do so. And who would believe it if old Auntie Minnie, who'd lived and died in the same small village, going nowhere and doing nothing out of the ordinary throughout her entire life, suddenly started spouting politics or great mystical truths through some random medium? Inspiration and wisdom have always been available to the living from within ourselves, *and* from outside sources. It isn't up to our deceased relatives and friends to proffer mind-blowing enlightenment; it is up to us, whilst here in the physical world, to seek it out for ourselves.

Having said that, souls *do* occasionally come out with interesting little nuggets of information that prove to be unnervingly true! I remember one consultation in which the customer's mother communicated that two people were going to lose their lives on the road, locally, and very soon. I was surprised by the message, to say the very least, as was the woman's daughter. I seriously questioned myself, wondering if, for some weird reason, I had just cooked that one up in my head. However, the consultation took place on a Tuesday... on the following Friday, whilst driving the children to school, we found that the road had been closed off by the police. Two young men travelling to work by car had been involved in an accident - and sadly, both were killed. I remember thinking, "oh my God... she was right", and feeling shaken to the core. Okay, you could argue that it was just a huge coincidence, but bear in mind that I live in a rural area and not a town or a city in which accidents occur daily. And, some might even suggest that such a prediction was the work of the 'dark side', but I wouldn't agree.

I don't know why that *particular* lady delivered the message; she had no connection (that I know of) to either of the young men. However, I understood what was being expressed: that things happen *before* they happen - if you see what I mean. The fact that the two young men were going to be in a certain place at a certain time, and take certain actions that would lead to a certain outcome, was already in motion... every last second of it. Yes, an *extremely* terrifying thought - but also incredibly mind-blowing! It shows that there *is* a much bigger picture at play here than we mortal souls tend to consider, under 'normal' circumstances. Of course, it is very possible that at any point leading up to the accident one or both of them could have made a last-minute change of plan, leading to a different outcome... but it was obviously 'known' that unfortunately this wasn't going to be the case.

It is our own personal belief about death, and life after death, that will influence our overall response to this story. Of course, first and foremost, we are going to feel incredibly sorry for the families of the two boys; after all, it is they who are left behind, they who will miss their beloved one every day of their lives. If we believe that death is wrong, is a dark and lonely place, and that God should only take the bad ones, then we will view all of this with fear and loathing... denial, even. If, however, we genuinely believe that physical life is one tiny but meaningful link in a possibly endless chain, and part of something *much* greater than our current existence, we will still feel sad - fearful even - but not defeated or helpless. We will still miss our deceased loved ones with every ounce of our being until it is our own time to go, but we will know for sure that love, being the most powerful force of all, doesn't just dissipate and disappear like smoke up a chimney. *They* may have finished experiencing this particular part of their existence but *we* haven't - *yet.* The tough part is not the dying; it is the remaining *until.* That's the bit that requires the most courage - that's the real challenge. And so, when customers would come to me seeking reassurance that the one who had died was 'alright', I would often say, "well, they're fine... but the big question is, what about *you*?"

Quickly going back to the story, over the following two years one of the young men (whose name begins with the letter M) showed up in several different consultations and I got to know him quite well! He had a nice way about him and was popular. He communicated that his parents had become very bitter, telling his friend's parents that they blamed *their son* for the loss of their own, even though he too had died. No-one could judge them, of course, and no-one would ever want to be in their shoes. Some people cope with grief better than others and that's all that can be said.

So, do all of the little stories I have just recounted here prove or explain anything about what happens to us beyond our physical death? No, not really. But they suggest that conscious awareness continues to exist even after the brain and the body has ceased to function. And, that basic communication between what could be called different dimensions of existence *is* possible, through the means of thoughts, feelings, and sensations. I never doubted any of that when I was working as a medium but I desperately wanted to see more of the bigger picture! Accepting that conscious awareness doesn't die with the body is only the tiniest tip of an immeasurable iceberg... and it wasn't enough for me! What *are* we aware of when we pass from this world? What do we *become*? What do we *do*? And do we actually continue to progress, and if so, *how*? These, and other questions, endlessly bounced around inside my head, pushing me to seek greater understanding. It made no sense to me that, following the amazing, strenuous, sometimes arduous, uncompromising, steep learning curve of life on Earth, the end result was an eternity of floating around in the sky with my also deceased relatives, looking down on the living, sending our love and telling them how happy and at peace we are with our new existence. I decided that if that is ALL there is, I'm not going... end of. In comparison, oblivion seemed attractive - at least I'd get a good long sleep!

However, something within me just knew for sure that that *wasn't* all there is... and even though there are billions of questions I will never have answers to, I believe that I *have* managed to put maybe one or two teeny-weeny jigsaw pieces into place (in a puzzle that has more parts than could ever be counted). Each of us may have our own puzzle that is unique and individual to us. We certainly all have our own beliefs, views, and opinions, especially where the subject of life after death is concerned. I have noticed, for example, whilst reading other writers' Amazon book reviews, that some people become incredibly upset when God is mentioned, others are offended because God or religion *isn't* mentioned, and some state that they already know *exactly* what happens beyond death and that the author is wrong. And, I myself came to learn that not everyone actually *wants* to question *or* be exposed to other people's questioning; it bothers and unsettles them. And they are, of course, at liberty to feel that way.

One such occasion took place in a large town hall which was hosting an evening of mediumship. Over the years I have performed on stage many, many times, before deciding that it was something I no longer wanted to do. My friend and I had seen this event advertised and we decided to go along. I was becoming a bit jaded and I think I was hoping that I would feel refreshed... maybe learn something I didn't know, or even pick up a tip or two.

We were the first to arrive, equipped ourselves with a G & T from the bar, and settled down to enjoy the evening. Thirty minutes in I realised that I was paying more attention to the audience of around 120 people than I was to the lady on stage. I was fascinated by their facial expressions and body language. Some appeared to be entranced, whilst others were yawning and fidgeting. It was enlightening to experience the process from the hall, rather than from the stage!

I suddenly became aware that the medium was explaining to us that when children die, they grow up in 'spirit'. I noticed that some people were keenly nodding in agreement. She then asked if anyone had any questions; I did, and I raised my hand.

"Do you believe in reincarnation?"

She smiled and responded with an emphatic, "Yes, I do!"

I had another question.

"And you also believe that children continue to grow up after they die?"

Again she was emphatic. "Absolutely!"

Hmm... okay, *now* I had to ask *another* question.

"Could you explain how the two beliefs are compatible with one another? If you believe in reincarnation then you believe that the soul is experienced and not *new*; it is the *body* that is new, enabling that soul to *revisit* the physical dimension. Because of death the new body is no longer functioning and the revisit is concluded. If the soul *is* an old, experienced one, then what age or stage does it actually grow up *to*?"

She went around the houses, not really answering, and when I said that I didn't understand what she was saying she snapped, "I'm only repeating what I've been taught!". Some members of the audience were glaring at me, willing me to shut my big mouth… which I did. After all, they too had paid to see this lady and didn't appreciate someone creating distractions. I understood.

I genuinely wasn't attempting to undermine the medium but I really wanted to hear her explanation. She'd asked for questions and I had put mine to her. I was initially baffled by the irritation of those around me until it clicked with me: they were *comfortable* with their beliefs about children and death, and they didn't want those beliefs to be challenged. I almost wished that I had kept my questions to myself. I didn't *want* to go around upsetting others… but that evening reminded me that neither did I want to continue working in a way that didn't feel right to *me*. Maybe the medium went home that night asking bigger questions of herself; maybe some of the audience members did the same. Maybe none of them did. Questions can open up doors that can lead to and open up even bigger doors (to the *unknown*, gulp!); sometimes we just want to keep those doors not only firmly closed and locked but boarded up too!

Now, you might ask why I can't just leave well alone? Why I don't settle on a set of beliefs and have done with it? Or, just walk away from the whole bloody subject and forget about it? Well, because one day *I* am going to die… and because I am completely sure that my life before and after death are inextricably linked… that one follows on from the other as part of an ongoing process. Some will say, "oh, I'm not going to waste my time worrying about what happens after I pop my clogs… I have to live for today."

Well, I'm *not* worrying. But, having peeked through the tiniest of gaps in the door to the 'afterlife', I am stuck with it; that door can no longer be closed. Having seen deceased people I have never met and didn't even know existed, giving snippets of meaningful information to living people I have only j*ust* met or spoken to, requires further consideration. It is *important.*

Our Life Beyond Death - An Incredible Journey

is available in paperback and Amazon Kindle.

Printed in Great Britain
by Amazon

61488812R00080